Breakthrough

by

Rebecca Clark

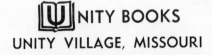
UNITY BOOKS
UNITY VILLAGE, MISSOURI

Foreword

Breakthrough . . . I like the sound and action of that word! I feel sure that you will experience many breakthroughs into your real nature as you read this inspiring and refreshing book by Rebecca Clark, especially if you read it with both heart and mind. So, read with joyful anticipation! As you take the words into yourself, the invisible living energy radiated from them will stir the creative potential of your whole being.

Actually, *Breakthrough* is more of a creative process than it is a book. Each chapter begins with an attunement activity and closes with a consciousness-conditioning program to help incorporate the ideas into a permanent pattern of self-expression and experience. Take your time with this book—assimilate its words, ideas, and courses of action into your heart, soul, mind, and body; into your rest, relaxation, and meditation; into your relationships, work, and play. Do this and you will be moved into a healthier, happier, richer, more adventurous way of living.

And you will know through actual experience that . . .

It's great to be alive!

J. Sig Paulson

CONTENTS

Preface

Ever since man began to think about his past and try to understand the tangled threads of progress, countless theories have evolved of his origin. Even in this enlightened age of space travel and atomic energy, the early stages in each onward course of human development are approached through a shadowy twilight that results in more diligent seeking. Occasionally the light of illumination touches mankind and we are spurred forward, ever seeking more answers, ever seeking what lies beyond our present awareness.

Institutions of home, government, and religion are known to us only in their present evolved forms. The rude beginnings of these cultures are buried beneath rubbish heaps of time. Those faraway centuries in which directive forces were forming the incipient movements that have culminated in what we call "our advanced civilization," are now fondly termed the Dark Ages.

It is impossible for us to look into the seeds of time and foretell which seeds will grow and produce and which seeds will not. The great movements and civilizations of the future are being planned, and the first faltering steps toward the realization of these plans are now being taken.

As the present is heir to the past, so will the future be the child of the present. We can either fear the future and hope for a stroke of luck or we can make a conscious effort to build our future, which means that we work today with a positive attitude and shape the future as we want it to be when we face it. Our future is assured if we work diligently and sincerely today, but it remains uncertain if we live aimlessly.

We do not live in a time of decline, but in a time of transition. Riots, crime, race problems, and fluctuating stock markets may cause the world to seem at odds and appearances may seem hopeless to some persons. But even the darkest night is followed by a new day, this new age—an age that some scientists, philosophers, and psychics call "golden."

The shocks and upheavals of our time are the storms of a tonic spring which can sweep away what is decayed to make room for the new. These are but the labor pains of a new era. The new age needs and wants to bring forth a new race of men and women who are strong and supreme because they are united in one cause—mankind's evolution.

Yes, we are in the process of change. We have strife and we often make tragic errors. But there is also growing strength—an unused inner strength that wants to break forth and that precedes great possibilities. Just as the powers from the depth of the earth push violently to the surface in volcanoes, so are great powers and abilities coming to light in souls who have been shaken by suffering and want to overcome, and who have had to overcome the greatest obstacles.

The restless and searching spirit of man, inspired by faith and hope in the divine order of the universe, will yet bring to power and dominion the living principles of international brotherhood and service to mankind. Surely future generations will say, "While it was yet dark, we discerned the birth throes of a new world order of peace and harmony!"

And this new order will be brought about by the most sturdy of all species—mankind. Every human being is a living dynamo of power and ability—a dynamo that, when unleashed, manifests itself in extraordinary ways for the benefit of all humanity. Every interested person should become an active student of life and learn by applying his newly gained knowledge to everyday situations. If we believe the Einstein theory which states that the average person uses less than one-tenth of his brain power, then do we dream an impossible dream? I think not!

An unprecedented flow of discoveries and an amazing accumulation of new knowledge slowly open the door for human advancement on the next great frontier of man's expanding knowledge—*self-awareness*. Perhaps our "coming of age" will be the major development of the twenty-first century, and through advanced knowledge and intensified study by individuals such as you and me, more people will use the tremendous assets in their latent abilities.

A new world does not just happen in the outer manifestation; it comes first from within each one of us. A better future must be born from our inner desire to progress. Great and magnificent possibilities of this future are waiting for our affirmation and unfoldment. We have within us the power to bring forth new life from the ruins and confusions of our times. We can be stronger than anything that distresses, grieves, or limits us. We must recognize and affirm this realization through courageous daily action. We must clear the way for this future and help to build it.

My purpose in writing this book is two-fold: First, I love our Earth. It is a place where majestic mountains, covered with stately trees, tower above daisy-splattered meadows; jagged soaring peaks reach up and brush the clouds; golden sands of vast reaches of desert flow toward sky-blue waters. Earth is a place where birds sing, animals and children play, men and women live, love, and work together. The sun shines and rain falls. Earth is our home, and I love it.

Second, I would like to perform whatever part is allowed to me for bringing to others the awareness of their own spiritual abilities. *You, dear soul, are a vital part of the divine arrangement of this great universe.* The confining walls of your life can roll back and there, spread before you like a banquet, are the greatest treasures life can offer.

Think of it! The same tremendous power that flows like a gigantic river through great cities is at your fingertips. Think of the changes you can bring about within your own sphere of life and operation. Think of the ever-flowing reservoir of cosmic power, so tremendously beautiful and staggering that your most abundant dreams and desires pale beside it!

You must make the first move and take the first step toward tapping this great reservoir. You have a right to happiness. Your dream may be to own a comfortable home or to have greater security. Perhaps you need additional money, or your satisfaction may come through achieving a true and lasting love relationship. All these things can be yours if you first find the knowledge and understanding necessary to make them a reality.

You do not have to be a common person. It is *your divine right* to be uncommon, for you are a child of God and heir to everything good and true. You can seek opportunity. You can take the calculated risks to dream and to build and to succeed! Accept the challenge of life and experience the thrill of divine fulfillment.

It is your heritage to stand erect and unafraid, to think and act for yourself, to enjoy the benefits of your growing awareness, and to face the world boldly and say, *"I can and I will accomplish my heart's true desire, for I am a child of God."*

In today's rapidly moving world, the sincere seeker wants to grow as quickly as possible. *True growth takes time.* It cannot be rushed and there are no shortcuts. I have tried in this book to condense the knowledge and training methods that I have acquired through many years of diligent study. These techniques are effective when studied and applied in daily life and they will enable your true spiritual nature to unfold. Then you will become master over your life and affairs.

You must learn to understand your own physical and spiritual nature before you can work successfully with your mind. You must know *what* and *who* you are. Permit that spark of divinity burning deep within your soul to ignite the wonderful you that is waiting for and seeking development.

Keep this book in a handy place. Thoroughly study the methods and procedures outlined in it, underline the points that are important to you, list your goals, and keep a record of your progress. Apply these teachings in your daily life. Before working with each chapter, take a few minutes to read the attunement exercise. Let the meaning of these words flow over your soul, opening new avenues of awareness as you attune your mind to the rhythm of the cosmos.

God bless you in your studies!

R. C.

Breakthrough

I

What's It All About?

Attunement

There is but one race: the human race.
There is but one man: God-man.
There is but one life: God-life.
There is but one mind: God-Mind.
There is but one Way: God's way.
There is but one goal: success!

The Search Begins

Almost everyone will agree that there is a Divine Mind, a supreme intelligence, tremendous and powerful, that conceives all things. Almost everyone will also agree that this powerful Consciousness is without beginning or end.

Although countless ages have come and gone, man has not learned exactly why he was created. Was it because the Creator loved the world which He had brought into being and desired to enjoy His own work? If so, He gave a part of Himself to the vital life forces that He directed to our planet Earth.

We realize that this divine force is everywhere present. It is present in the simple beauty of a field daisy and in the complexity of a majestic rose. The sea anemone vibrates with the same essence of vital life force as does a pet dog or cat. We also realize that this divine essence is present in every living person regardless of race, color, belief, and location, and regardless of whether or not we like the person. Admittedly, some persons find it hard to realize the divine Presence in someone they don't like, although they can easily spot goodness in the people they love.

It is a fact that the divine Presence of the universe dwells within every individual. The only barrier which could ever seemingly separate you from the tender loving care of the Infinite is you, your own failure to understand or learn how to take advantage of the precious gift you hold.

If it were within your ability to arrange your life in a smooth and orderly progression, to obtain an abundance of the bountiful life treasures which are your divine right, wouldn't it be worthwhile to put forth strong effort toward achieving this goal? Wouldn't you direct your conscious thoughts toward uniting with this divine Presence?

Choosing the Best Way

All the things you are seeking are perfectly natural and are seeking you! Other persons who have reached a certain degree of evolution have realized this, and it is possible for you to reach this wonderful state of evolvement. But one thing is vitally important: *you will never obtain something for nothing.* Our universe simply does not work that way. There is no "climbing over the wall," there is no "crashing or storming" the gates of heaven, for the gates open only to those who have traveled the path of purification and dedication, and who have sincerely walked the path of service and love. Wishes and desires and intellectual knowledge alone will not do it. A "breakthrough" in consciousness is needed; the breakthrough that leads to initiation into higher levels of intelligence and spiritual perception.

Realizing the Truth

Yogi Ramacharaka presented some important concepts in his book, "The Life Beyond Death." They are worth repeating here:

"There are three great truths which are absolute, and which cannot be lost, but yet may remain silent for lack of speech. (1) The soul of man is immortal, and its future is the future of a thing whose growth and splendor have no limit. (2) The principle which gives life dwells in us, and without us; is undying and eternally beneficent; is not heard or seen, or felt, but is perceived by the man who desires perception. (3) Each man is his absolute law-giver; the dispenser of glory or gloom to himself, the decreer of his life, his reward, his punishment.

"These truths, which are as great as life itself, are as simple as the simplest mind of man. Feed the hungry with them."

Have you ever felt the gnawing way down deep inside that causes you to think, "I'm hungry," yet you do not have a physical hunger? Have you ever experienced that particular restlessness that makes you wonder what life is really all about? Are you hungry for Truth? Are you hungry for knowledge and growth? If so, you are feeling the hunger pangs of the inner needs of man—needs which prompt him to seek the hidden knowledge that gives true meaning to life.

Are you hungry for Truth? Are you hungry for knowledge and growth? The food is yours for the taking! Let the cosmic law that *you* are responsible for your life bring the first faint glimmer of understanding and help you to plant your feet firmly on the grand path to achievement. Nothing good or bad has ever happened in your life that you did not consciously or unconsciously bring upon yourself. Trying to shift responsibility to others doesn't solve problems; this is only an unsuccessful attempt to deceive yourself. Until you are ready to accept the fact that you are responsible for your life, you are as vulnerable as the autumn leaves tossed about by the wind.

Many people have remarked to me, "Oh, you say that, but you don't know all the problems I have had!"

Of course I don't know what their problems have been, but I have grown to realize and understand that no one has ever been in a tragic spot or experienced desperate needs unless there was some noncompliance with universal law at a previous point. This same noncompliance in each instance was inharmony with the true nature of his beingness.

All right, so where do you go from here? You are beginning to realize the responsibility you have to yourself. You want to begin making attunement with the presence of God and start making the way a lot smoother. How do you do this?

Three Basic Steps

1. This first step is very important. *Keep an open mind.* Maintain an unbiased and completely unprejudiced point of view. Just because others may think differently than you do, doesn't necessarily mean either of you is right—or wrong. Listen. Learn. Forget your own immediate environment, your ego or personality. Simply become a human being representing the vital life force of all human life in the divine process of evolution. Try to assume a vantage point above and beyond the earth plane. Then look backward toward earth and look out into the great cosmic realm of the spiritual universe. Analyze everything and try to realize the Truth as it touches you.

2. *Accept the fact* that you can learn to control your destiny by controlling the circumstances surrounding your life. Control your health. Control your position in life. Control your prosperity. Control your spiritual growth. The universe has an infinite capacity of givingness for you, but you must develop your capacity to receive and use its gifts.

3. *Realize* the fact that everything you or I or anyone else could ever need is available. Perhaps you haven't received your bounty yet and feel it is long overdue, but it is there for your asking. Just because you haven't reached up and claimed your divine heritage from God doesn't change the Truth.

When you look at another person, you see another physical body. You see the color of his hair and eyes. You see whether he is short or tall, slim or heavy, and all the physical characteristics that combine to complete that person. When he speaks you hear the sound of his voice. It might be soft and pleasant or it might be harsh and grating. That person is alive, but what you don't see is the spark of life animating his body, his voice, and his thoughts.

In addition to this vital life force, you are given fantastic tools with which to work. You have a mentality and an emotional nature. It is the combination of your given mentality and your emotional nature (or subconscious mind), following *your* direction toward accomplishing a specific task, which makes your life what it is at this moment.

You and I, through our deliberate thinking, have the power of selecting what we will think, and it is through this deliberate selection and directed thought process that we begin to mold, control, and put to good use our emotional nature. Remember what was mentioned earlier? Nothing bad has ever happened to you that did not result from your own violation of divine law. Nothing good has ever happened to you that did not result from your harmonious compliance, although perhaps on an unconscious level, with divine law.

Analyze the inharmonies in your life. If you are honest with yourself, you will admit most illnesses are spawned by the impact of negative emotions—hurts and fears and angers—that penetrated deeply into the subconscious mind and remained there. As these emotions remained buried underground, they festered and grew, spreading their poison throughout your system until the body reacted. As a result, you became ill. Uproot these negative seeds from your thoughts. Refuse to allow them to grow.

How do you do this? Use the thought power of the

great infinite Mind which created everything and which is within you! We are told in the Bible that God created man after His own image, His own thinking and likeness. We are also told that He gave man dominion over the earth. Use your power of dominion! How do you ask for realization of this marvelous power? Let me give you an example.

One morning I was driving to the shopping center for groceries. It was a glorious spring day and I felt "on top of the world" and very appreciative of the lavish natural beauty all around. The tree-lined street was quiet except for some noisy blue jays. Sunlight filtered through the thick leaves of maple trees and the pink and white blossoms of dogwoods along the sidewalk, making bright reflections.

Perhaps it was the glare of sunlight which prevented the driver of another car from seeing my vehicle. He was approaching the main street upon which I was traveling, and just as I entered the intersection, he looked neither right nor left, but pulled directly into the path of my car. I jammed down my brake pedal, but stopping was impossible.

"God, help!" I cried at what seemed certainly the moment of impact.

The next few seconds were incredible. My car was gently halted and the other car seemed to be literally pushed from my path. Somehow we passed by each other without the seemingly inevitable accident. The other driver didn't stop and as his car roared down the street, I drove to the curb and sat for a few minutes with the car motor idling (and my motor going full speed), trying to relax, and repeatedly saying, "Thank You, God!" My frantic plea for help had been heard and answered immediately.

Always before giving a lecture or performing a service, I pause and ask God to take over and guide my thoughts, actions, and words so they may be of benefit to others. Then, I sit quietly for a few minutes and give the response a chance to pour into my heart and soul. A feeling of such peace and tranquillity flows over me at these times that I *know* I am not alone. And that presents another opportunity to say, "Thank You!"

It really doesn't matter what your problem or situation is, the application is always the same: give the spiritual forces an opportunity to come through for you and you will be amazed to see how insecurity is crowded out by the feeling of confidence and security. Maintain a childlike faith, simplicity of heart, clear-thinking mind, and complete trust in God. Know that the hidden power within your being is the same force that created and sustains the universe. By realizing this Truth, you become aware of a second great gift from the Creator—besides the gift of life, you also have the gift of thought.

How You Can Use the Gift of Thought

Use the wonderful gift of thought to your best advantage. It is easy to realize that the presence of God within us denotes perfect health, perfect vitality, and abundant energy. Therefore, if you are ill, it is logical that you have become separated from this Presence in some way. It is so easy to bring yourself back into complete harmony by just remembering that the Presence of God the Creator, residing within you, is perfect and you are created in His image and likeness.

When you truly believe this, nothing in the world can overpower you. If anything of a lower or denser nature should try to touch you, you can dispense with it so quickly you will hardly realize the contact.

The Neglected Gift

If someone gave you a magnificent birthday present and you tucked it away in a closet or drawer and never opened it, what good would it bring to you? If someone gave you a luxurious new car, with the stipulation you must pick up the keys at the factory, dust would billow from your heels as you hastened to claim your gift. You wouldn't think of neglecting to claim the car. Yet, this is exactly what most persons are doing with the greatest gift in the world—they are neglecting to claim it!

The Creator's supreme gift to you is the ability to arrange your life into the happy, attuned existence it should be.

Discover this marvelous gift buried within yourself. Use it to strengthen your dormant spiritual muscles. Put these muscles to work for you. Perhaps certain of your faculties have been sleeping. These faculties can be awakened and developed to an even greater extent than is necessary in developing the muscle and nerve centers in your fingers and hands in order to demonstrate a physical skill.

Practice Makes Perfect

If you have ever attempted to master any of the arts—painting, playing a musical instrument, sewing, or doing anything that requires a certain amount of dexterity—you realize practice is necessary. You must awaken, educate, and whip into efficiency certain functions and faculties of the mind, the nervous system, and the muscles which have not been trained before. Nature requires a certain length of time in training before these functions and faculties, nerves and muscles can become familiar with the activities required of them.

When performing growth experiments, the success and efficiency of what you do depends not only upon your muscles and nerve centers, but also upon awakening the spiritual centers of your body.

Regardless of how well you may understand a principle or a law and its application, until the proper function or faculty within you is developed to a state of responsiveness, you cannot accomplish the task you attempt.

Wake Up to a Wonderful New World

The results of your application will be a "new you." The first thing that will happen is that your whole organism will begin to transform into a healthy specimen. You will begin to feel like a completely new person. Instead of greeting each new day with groans, you will be cheerfully saying, "Good morning, God!"

Welcome each new day. It is another glorious opportunity for you. It is a thrilling new experience and a happy adventure in soul growth. You will find the sky becoming brilliantly blue . . . the trees and grass an *alive* green . . . and every creation of nature radiating an effervescent glow. No, nothing has changed—except *you*. You are beginning to see the work of the Creator through His eyes, and it is good. It is very good!

To learn the truth about the great cosmic universe, first learn the truth about yourself. Explore your home, your neighborhood, your town, your nation, and finally, the whole wonderful world. Knowledge is like a sparkling, cheerful fire which warms and brightens everything in a room. Knowledge and understanding, working together, can help you become an expert in human (and you-man) relations. There is pure magic in such insight. The experience of David T. is excellent evidence.

David was having difficulties with a worker under his supervision who created chaos and disharmony in the office. Deliberate disturbances, aimed at testing David's authority kept him on edge and relations strained. This was even more upsetting since the worker supposedly was a good friend of his, although an envious one. But David was an unusual person when it came to dealing with life's little blows. He was deeply interested in cosmic enlightenment and had been studying for several years. Now was the time to put the knowledge he had gained into practice.

First, David quietly surveyed the situation. He realized he had allowed himself to be mentally wounded by his friend's actions. This reaction was wrong because it was self-damaging. So David began to put the problem in its proper perspective. He decided he must let this problem fall upon his understanding and not upon his ego.

The source of the problem was plain to him. His friend had a bad case of insecurity and was venting his own frustrations upon everyone else. David wanted to help but he also recognized the fact that each person has to find his own avenue of growth. Yet, something had to be done.

David called a private conference with his friend. It was a painful procedure but it proved worthwhile. David honestly analyzed the problem involved and the consequences that must follow if certain rules and regulations were not observed. He also offered his helpful friendship and understanding in whatever way was needed. His friend was dumbfounded. Here was a man who had been the brunt of deliberate harassment and who was now offering sincere friendship, offering to help, piercing right through his shield of pretense and still believing in him. It seemed crazy! But David knew what he was doing.

Several weeks passed without incident and the things discussed during the meeting began to sink slowly beneath the surface and touch a tender spot of self-analysis in the worker. The things David had said began to make sense. The results? A potentially good employee was converted into a good employee. A tormented soul began to see a faint glimmering of the light and understanding in himself, thus realizing that he was not alone in his moments of anguish and insecurity.

Believe in Yourself

Believe in yourself! Believe you were made and meant to perform any task without calling for aid from anyone. Without growing too scornfully proud, believe that you are endowed with as much as the greatest person who has ever lived. You have a marvelous mind to do thinking, two hands and feet and eyes and ears, and all the tools God gives to the wise.

You are divinely designed and perfectly meant for the work of mankind. Whatever heights man has reached, you can also reach. Whatever success has been attained, you can also attain.

You are the radiant, all-wise, all-loving, all-conquering child of God. A new day is here to be experienced—a day filled with wonderful hours, ready to reveal their particular treasures. Be open. Be receptive.

Oh, beautiful and eternal child of God, *know your worth*.

You are important. If God cradles the tiny sparrows in His loving, everlasting arms, will He not do likewise with you—His beloved child? You are necessary in the overall scheme of life. And life will never abandon you; it will continue to experience through you in all forms and levels. Just as each shiny sunbeam has its special spot of the earth to caress with warmth and light, and every lovely leaf has its own area to shade, so do you have your unique place to fill, to bless, and to give of your very best.

You are important. Put away false ideas of smallness and allow life's greatness to fill your individuality. Grow and expand in Spirit continually from horizon to horizon. Begin now to grow beyond your current knowledge. The richness of the past and the excitement of the future are merging into your awareness of the present. Allow the completeness to happen. Know your true worth, and let the peace that comes from perfect understanding flood your beautiful soul and reflect radiantly on every other person you meet. Open your life to the life that created it.

Experience this life in all its glorious wonder— sometimes incomprehensible, occasionally a little frightening, but overall, exciting, fulfilling, and good.

If things don't always work as well as they should and there are many temptations to try to pull you back, return to the realization that you have erred somewhere along the way. Then turn yourself and your situation over to God to be set right again. And you will *know* exactly what steps to take.

You will develop a new and good outlook toward your fellowmen. There is not one of us who does not come in constant contact with other people. You will learn to treat others as you desire to be treated. If at first the reaction to your sunshine and warmth is lacking, or seems that way, don't lose faith. *Persevere!* Keep on transmitting love and happiness and soon you will begin living this tremendous concept of life. You will find you *are* becoming that wonderful vehicle of positive and constructive thinking, kindness, understanding, faith, and love.

Remember, if you don't feel immediate response from your first attempts to grow in cosmic consciousness, don't give up. After all, a baby must crawl for several months before taking the first shaky steps.

This is the period where so many good "potentials" fall by the wayside, just short of success. Every effort you exert toward learning *does* produce growth and results, even though you may not be able to feel the progress you have made. This is the time to hang on, to build your faith. You can do it. Everyone can do it!

The words of the prayer, "Lord, let there be peace on earth, and let it begin with me," are so vital. If love and peace begin with me and I spread them to you, then you in turn spread them to those you know; it becomes infectious. With this kind of chain reaction, we can truly live in a world of universal harmony. We have enough of a nucleus among us to spread success. Not one of us realizes just how many people we know. And if everyone "spread the word," what a miracle we would experience within a short time.

Now, let's get on with learning some of the important stepping-stones on the path toward obtaining cosmic consciousness.

Consciousness Conditioners

1. Universal forces are already within you. Learn how to use them successfully and positively.
2. Recognize that everything you have always wanted, also wants you.
3. *Practice awareness.* Look around you and see, hear, feel, and enjoy the gifts life is offering, then share them with others.
4. *Love truth above all else.* Be real. Leave off the superficialities.

5. Remember that one of your best teachers is daily experience.
6. When progress seems slow, keep polishing your spiritual abilities. *Persistence* pays off.
7. Always put universal laws and principles ahead of man-made codes.
8. Remember that nothing external can overshadow you when you *realize the power of God within you.*
9. You cannot expect to receive great blessings if you spend only moments each day in affirming what you want and the rest of the time in foolish and unproductive thoughts.
10. *You are a child of God.* Go forth from this moment and act like one!

II

Training the Soul

Attunement

The entire universe is a mystery, and man's inquisitive mind thrives on a challenge. If we accept the challenge of our existence and take the time to search for the key to unlock the secrets, we can discover and uncover the mystery of God, life, and our place in it!

The Mystery of Life

What is it that makes the difference between a tiny ant and the small grains of sand the ant uses to build the little mound around its hole in the earth? It isn't merely cell construction, but something in the cells themselves.

What is it that enables an animal of microscopic dimensions, after having been frozen in antarctic ice for years, to resume activity as soon as the ice melts? It is the marvel called life.

What is it that makes the infinitesimal mustard seed sprout and grow into a mature tree? It is that same mystery and marvel called life.

What is it that makes John Doe so different after physical death takes place? It isn't anything regarding the structure of the cells of his body, but something that was once in those cells and is now gone from them—something vitally important, the principle of life—*the vital life force.*

And just what is this vital life force? What is the quality or character distinguishing an animal or plant from inorganic or dead bodies? Life is that expression of God which manifests as animation, activity, vigor. Life is the acting principle acting upon substance. Life is that marvelous energy that propels all forms to action. Science can tell us all *about* life, but it is helpless in answering the questions of what it is that *makes* life.

It can only be said that life is something given. It is an endowment from God. It is a unique experience. Life is that glorious "something" that enables us to be what we are: sentient beings, capable of voluntary motion, thought, feeling, action, growth, reproduction, and mental, moral, and spiritual desires. Beyond that we cannot go. No one can tell essentially what life is or how it began to manifest after the earth ceased to be a whirling ball of gas and fire.

Creative Evolution

What a fantastic piece of creation is man. How noble in ideals. How infinite in faculties. How strong in aspiration. How *naive* in awareness.

Man is here, right now. Man is present in this time and space. The question is one of present goals, not one of origin. What is man reaching toward? What is man's manifest destiny? Every person alive feels the struggle going on within himself, like a warfare between the flesh and the spirit. He feels within himself the demands of the animal beast, but he also feels within him the upward pull, the clarion call of his higher being.

We would not turn to a tiger who is about to eat someone and strike the tiger on the head and say, "Brace up! Be a tiger!" (That is exactly what the tiger is being.) But whenever we see man becoming beastlike we should desire to touch him on the shoulder and say, "Brace up! Be a man!" We should tingle with moral responsibilities. We should be eager for more abundant life. We should ever seek opportunities for growth. We should continually reach out into the universe and strive for greater awareness of our own reality and of the reality of God.

God is not in the remote past, having created man and let him go full speed ahead at his own initiative. Nor is God in the distant future waving a beckoning finger, urging man forward in a struggle under his own power. God is within each one of us. He is within all life, compelling life, moving it onward and upward, and moving man to realize within himself that divine life of which he is now only faintly aware.

An ancient king was seated in his garden and one of the king's counselors spoke to him of the wonderful works of God.

"Show me a sign," said the king, "and I will believe."

"Well, here are four acorns," said the counselor. "Will your majesty plant them in the ground and then lean forward and gaze into the clear pool of water?"

The king did as requested.

"Now, look up," requested the counselor. The king looked up and gasped in astonishment at forty oak trees which stood straight and strong where the acorns had been planted.

"Oh, this is wonderful!" exclaimed the king. "This is indeed the work of God!"

"How long were you gazing into the pool of water, sire?" asked the counselor.

"Only a few seconds," replied the king.

And then the counselor answered, "No, sire, eighty years have passed as though a second."

The king looked at his garments, now worn and tattered. Then he leaned forward and stared at his reflection in the clear water of the pool. It was true. He was a very old man.

"Then," said the king, "this is no miracle at all. God did not do it, nature did."

How true it is that seeming miracles, when looked at with eyes of understanding, become perfect manifestations of the natural law of the universe in action. Must God perform miracles to be God? Do we need physical proof of the miracle of man? Are we to lose the sense of wonder in creation because of vast stretches of time? Is God some petty magician who must startle us and surprise us in order to be effective? Or is God the loving Creator in whom we live, move, and have our being all the way along the journey of life?

Ours is a creative evolution. To conceive of God as being outside of His universe—as a sculptor, a molder, an infinite artisan—is a defective conception of God. God is not only transcendent, He is also immanent.

His center is everywhere; His circumference is nowhere! He is within every assemblage of crystals, within every movement of life, whether it be animal, vegetable, or mineral. God is working out His creation, His purposes, until at last there stands upon the face of planet Earth a creation called man—God Himself manifesting in human life.

How Alive Are You?

We may not know what life is, but we know a lot of things about it. Some people seem to be more vitally alive than others. We have learned, too, that our aliveness depends upon how we treat ourself and what we do with our strengths and powers. We know that our aliveness can be increased by proper rest and nourishment, by our activities, by our thoughts, feelings, and the manner in which we discipline ourself.

Not only is it desirable to develop abundant physical life, but as our spiritual life increases, so does everything about us intensify, becoming more vibrant, more glowing, more "alive." The spirit of man is like fire and from its very nature, tends to seek contact—vital, enlarging contact—with the eternal Spirit of God. The development of the soul-life depends not upon extraordinary endowment, but upon the intensity of desire, intelligent effort, and the deliberate release of latent inner possibilities.

And what is this soul we want to develop and train? It is man's consciousness, the underlying idea back of any expression. Our soul is comprised of the many accumulated ideas back of our present expression. In its original and true sense, the soul of man is the expressed idea of man in Divine Mind. Our body is soul expressing, and our soul includes the conscious and the subconscious levels of mind. Soul makes the body; our body is the outer expression of the soul.

We begin development or expansion of our soul through the unfoldment of divine ideals and the expression of these ideals in our body. The soul is fed by our thoughts and the old adage, "You are what you think!" is more true than we realize.

Therefore, *if physical life is a congenital endowment, then life of the Mind and Spirit is something that can be sought after and deliberately cultivated.* The soul can be trained as easily as the mind, and it needs to be trained.

Desire Is the First Step

Nothing worthwhile is ever accomplished without *desire*. A man who does not desire to reach the other side of a chasm will not likely do so even though he makes the leap. Within every person is the desire, however intense, for a more abundant, more vigorous, richer life for the soul. Yet it is up to each one of us to fan the flame of spiritual desire day in and day out to make it stronger. We must think about it so much that it becomes a blazing passion within us.

But desire alone is not enough. A distance runner who enters a race may have the desire to win, but he isn't likely to win unless he previously has given himself intense training. Regardless of how much you want something, of how much you have learned, of how far you have gone in pursuit of spiritual knowledge and the practice of what you have learned, there is still more progress to be made. Before further progress can be made, more knowledge is needed. In order to make the needed progress, it is necessary to give yourself definite training. Merely attending church or classes is not enough for developing a great life in the soul. We need knowledge of things to do, methods to pursue, habits to cultivate.

There are many stories of famous men and women who have disciplined themselves almost furiously in order to "destroy the power of the flesh" and make the great spiritual ascent. But the key is harmony and balance—the harmony and balance which results when *Spirit, soul, and body are brought into alignment and work in balanced manifestation.*

Without extraordinary psychic endowment of any kind, you can give your soul the spiritual training needed in order for you to come completely and abundantly into the fullness.

Why Not Try God?

Often I have heard the phrase, "When all else fails, try God." Well, why not start with God? Why not let the Truth of God be the master helmsman and let your course in life be charted straight and true to a rich and meaningful life?

Effort must go hand in hand with knowledge. Brother Lawrence emphasized the *practice* of the presence of God in every minute of every day of our life. This is the whole secret of a vital spiritual life. In order to *know* God, we must *think often* of God. And how can we think often of God unless we acquire the holy habit? This is simple down-to-earth fact, straightforward and without anything exceptional or artificial. The practice of God-awareness can become such a habit that it is carried into all the hours of the day.

We all are engaged in the task of building ourself into a stronger individual. There is nothing more or less in the sum of our habits—good and bad. Habits are found largely, not entirely, in the choice we make in little everyday things, things that often seem totally inconsequential. Our character governs our destiny and this is easily seen in what we are; and what we do depends on how we make our best choice in little things of life.

If you continue in life as you are right now, where will you be in ten years?

Decide right now that you want a fantastic life and refuse to accept anything less as a substitute. You are destined for greatness. Why accept a mundane existence when you can experience ecstasy?

We cannot vitally live with God for one part of the day, if we deliberately separate ourself from Him for another part of the day. In all the affairs and transactions of daily life, we must learn this Truth and concern ourself with being a co-worker with God.

The Art of Knowing

Have you ever watched a child take its first wobbly, insecure steps? The little legs move forward, hesitantly at first, and the child sometimes tumbles to the floor. But he continues to put forth effort and his steps gradually become more firm and effective.

The quest of the Spirit is also a growing process. It

is a training process. It requires steadfast effort and devotion. It requires *action* on your part. Start now to think of yourself as being everything you know you should be and want to be. Think of yourself right now as being gentle, loving, and kind to every man, woman, and child you meet, and to every circumstance life may bring your way. Think of yourself as being kind and tolerant in your attitudes toward all conditions on earth. Think of yourself as being an island of calm serenity in all conditions and under all circumstances, quiet and yet strong—strong with the strength to reach out a loving hand to seemingly weaker brothers and sisters, strong with the strength to speak the right words, to take the right actions, and to *become* an unshakable tower of strength and light.

See yourself facing any seeming injustice or unkindness with a beautifully serene spirit. See yourself *knowing* that all things will work out in time for the ultimate good of everyone. Begin knowing that justice is always triumphant if you can be patient and follow the process of the outworking of the magnificent will of God.

If you can begin to see yourself accomplishing some of these things, and begin to know that you have everything within you necessary to accomplish these things, you are well on the way toward training the soul and knowing something of mastership.

If you will remain steadfast on the path to which your feet have been guided, you will find the treasure of life—a treasure that brings abundance of every good thing life can offer. You have only to seek in simple trust and sincerity, and *you shall receive.* You have no need that cannot be gloriously supplied.

Redeeming the Body

We have been bound so long in the limitations of materiality that we often fail to identify ourself with our spirit and our soul, and often think of ourself only as a body. But light begins to dawn and the error becomes apparent. As a result, often in our zeal for getting back on the right track, we have gone to the other extreme and denied the body any place of importance. *It is important to wipe out all belief of separation in Spirit, soul, and body.*

This offspring of God, divine idea-man, must be recognized in every thought and word, so it may be manifested in completeness.

Let the idea of the body as just an earthly house be dissolved. Become clothed now with the divine idea of man complete. In this idea, you are one with the immortal, incorruptible flesh of the Christ and you have eternal life. Your body is truly the temple of the living God.

At this moment you are the sum total of every thought that has ever germinated and developed in your brain—and of every thought you have permitted to enter from without and find lodging within. As your life evolves you will continue to be more and more what you choose to make of yourself by the exercise of your thinking powers. *Now is the time for a great awakening.* See the glory and splendor you truly are. See the magnificent radiance of a soul training for ever-higher realms of expression and development. Refuse to accept less than the highest vision you can hold for yourself. You deserve the greatest level of attainment you can achieve, for you are a child of God. You are heir to everything in the universe. Claim your inheritance.

Getting Rid of the Garbage

Inside a computer can be found all kinds of configurations of data. We can bring new data in and change its form. We can twist it around, move it, and stick it in all sorts of little cubby-holes. The same thing happens in the computer inside our head. Because of our sloppy programming, we often bring our data in on one format and without properly processing it we try to read it in a different format. The result is mental garbage. Then we wonder why we have garbage manifesting in our life.

When we take a good analytical look at the mess in our life, we normally find that it is there because we did not handle the inputs properly. We did not change the formats before we tucked them away into neat little pigeonholes. Perhaps an experience in our day struck us as unhappy and negative, so we stored it that way in our mind, to fester and attract more discomfort.

The beautiful thing is that we can stop all this nonsense. We can quit taking the inputs of the physical or even the psychic senses directly into the system. We can bring them into a buffer area to look at, to analyze them, to check their validity, and to decide if the result is worth storing in our computer. We can test everything on the way in, *before* we treat it as a valid experience or idea. When we bump into an experience that is less than beautiful or good or uplifting—less than the kind of things we like and want to live with—we can give it that "invalid" punch and reject it, settling only for that which is good. We do our screening while the data is still in our buffered input stage, not after it gets filed with the "good" stuff. If we could practice one hundred percent positive thinking, imagine what control we would have over our life!

Ageless Soul, Regain Thy Youth

Ponce de Leon sought the fountain of youth—as most persons do. But alas! The majority seek in the wrong direction.

One day a man who was leading a busy, active, and useful life discovered quite by chance that he was sixty years old. This fact startled him and he began to relinquish perfectly good plans for doing meaningful work because he felt that there would not be enough time in his life to complete the works he wanted to do.

A friend who was aware of what was happening asked him one day, "How old is your mind?"

"Why, it isn't old. It is strong and wise and really quite intelligent. One's mind should be even better at sixty because of the years of experience in life."

Then the friend asked, "How old is your body?"

"My body is quite strong. I exercise daily and am involved with sports. Why, I am a great deal more active than men half my age."

"How old is your heart?" was the next question from the friend.

"I have the heart of a child!" exclaimed the man. "I love life and I love nature and I love people. But what does all this questioning have to do with the fact that I'm sixty years old?"

The friend replied, "If your mind is stronger than ever, and your body is more active than the bodies of many younger men, and you have the happy heart of a child, what is there about you that is sixty?"

The man could not answer.

The number of years that we have lived have nothing to do with the age of the soul. The soul is eternal. Youth is eternal. Youth is in the heart and the mind. Youth is Spirit and the soul is ageless. It is never too late to start training the soul.

Master Training Techniques

Someone once said, "Plans are the dreams of those who have understanding." We should choose rightly in whatever we wish to accomplish and then proceed with a plan. It is better to think before we act. If we want to be effective and successful, we must have a definite goal, proceed with a definite plan and in an orderly way. It is like building a house: everything must be planned carefully and each detail carried out until the house is completed.

Thinking, planning, and training today means mastery tomorrow.

All of life is a training course, and experience is something that is sometimes so harsh that only by the use of sheer willpower does man survive. But man does survive and if he learns, he grows. Every soul on earth is an unfinished product, subject to error. We are seeking to grow forward as rapidly as possible and with the least amount of error.

Where do you want to get in life? What is the first step? Why don't you take it now?

Be master of yourself.

Leading the Triumphant Life

Leading the triumphant life is the part we forget most frequently. We have been studying details, developing techniques, practicing, exercising, and there is really only one thing left to do: put what we have learned into daily practice. Without application, there is nothing. How often do we remember to apply and use? Is our newly acquired knowledge still an intellectual exercise or is it becoming a habit, with at least part of it put into use on a daily basis?

We live in a beautiful ocean of God's love, with abundance all around us. Are we remembering to pay attention to what floats by and decide what we should do about it? This brings us back to the point of balance in our own life and in the life of others. When we try to talk with people, they sometimes don't listen. What do we do then? There is only one answer they will accept. We have to let them make their own mistakes. *People will accept only what they want to accept.*

This is when the age-old idea of blessing and releasing comes into play. We lovingly bless others as children of God and release them to make their own decisions. And we pray that their decisions will be the right ones.

If we can hang on to the idea that we live in a vast

ocean of God's love, abundantly flowing with divine ideas, and if we will notice what is flowing by, then we may receive fresh clues toward making a better life.

I mentioned this ocean of God's love one day in a class and a student responded, "What happens if your boat sinks?" The old Navy adage popped into my mind, and I replied, "You take off your clothes and make water wings!"

You are being given many "water wings" in this book, so how about letting the reality of God's love for you, and your reality as a child of God, make you unsinkable?

Consciousness Conditioners

1. Life is that expression of God which manifests as *animation*, *activity*, and *vigor*. You are filled with it at this very moment. Recognize this reality and live.
2. How alive are you? Measure your "aliveness" by the intensity of your desire to really live.
3. All that the Father has is yours. Claim your inheritance.
4. Try God! You will be fantastically amazed at the marvelous results in your life.
5. Be sure of *what* you want from life and offer *twice* as much in return.
6. Courage to step forward to obtain a desired goal is one step closer to success.
7. Constancy of purpose is the first principle of success.
8. The most interesting thing about a postage stamp

is the remarkable persistency with which it sticks
to its job!

9. You're never too old, and it's never too late to
begin.
10. You and God—*an unbeatable team.* Remember
this.

III

Grand Cosmic Being

Attunement

Our Birth is but a sleep; and a forgetting:
The Soul that rises with us, our life's Star
Hath had elsewhere its setting,
And cometh from afar:
Not in entire forgetfulness,
And not in utter nakedness,
But trailing clouds of glory do we come
From God, who is our home.
                    —*William Wordsworth*

What Are You?

"I'm the child of a King,
        The child of a King . . . "
How beautiful are these words of affirmation taken from a favorite hymn that sings of God's truth of our being. How meaningful these words become when we take them into our life and affairs and truly *know* that we are children of a King—God, the greatest King!

How do we define God as a King? One definition of the word *king* is, "something supreme in its class."

God is supreme in His class—in fact, God is supreme in everything, for God is the Creator of all there is!

The relationship of God to man is the parent-child relationship; God created us, so we are His offspring. To create is to bring into being, to cause to exist. God's life-giving energy emanates throughout space, all conditions, and all things. It is not given to just one person or one group; it is all-in-all and it belongs to everyone, whether we realize it now or not.

Like the relationship of a parent and child, we are always a part of God and can never be separated from Him, the Source from which we had our beginning.

> I was crowned by my God, my crown is living . . .
> I received the face and the fashion of a new person . . .
> And the thought of truth led me on.
> I walked after it and did not wander.
> And all that have seen me were amazed and I was regarded by them as a strange person.
> And He who knew and brought me up is the Most High in all His perfection. And He gloried me by His kindness, and raised my thoughts to the height of His Truth.
> And from thence He gave me the way of His precepts and I opened the doors that were closed.
> And broke in pieces the bars of iron; but my iron melted and dissolved before me:
> Nothing appeared closed to me, because I was the door of everything.
>
> —Wisdom of Solomon

Why Are We Here?

Mankind came into the world to bring forth his God-likeness; that is, to express his own true nature which is *the Christ.* Enfolded within each person is the divine pattern, the glorious divine blueprint, or God's idea of the perfect person.

We should never allow false thoughts to enter our mind.

We should never feel that a person or a situation is difficult, for in this manner, we raise unnecessary obstacles to achieving our true purpose. Let all power rest in God. Regard all seeming obstacles as merely stones to be cast into the ocean of life—stepping-stones to the manifestation of greater glory. See the power and the glory of the risen *Christ consciousness* shining where seeming obstacles formerly dared to lodge.

We are gradually coming out of the mental darkness of our past beliefs into the light of understanding where we can now realize each one of us is an evolving soul, expanding in spiritual consciousness to have conscious union with God. As we move forward, we conquer the fear of death, illness, poverty, and loneliness. We begin to realize that we must do these things for ourself; no one else can do them for us. When Jesus conquered these mental attitudes for Himself, He made it possible for us to do likewise.

The experiences of our return to God-likeness are shown in our life and attitudes of today, and what we do today will shape our future destiny. Thus, let us regard life as one continuous process of evolution. The young soul comes into incarnation, evolves, expands, and strives ever forward until eventually it becomes a son of the living God in the essence of Truth. It has been learning lessons bravely and expanding all the time, not only in this present life, but in past life. The seeds sown in past lifetimes and in our yesterdays as negative thoughts, wrong passions, low desires are all garnered today as weeds and thistles. So we reap today what was sown in the past that has not yet been transmuted. But we have a blessed and great opportunity *now* to sow seeds of the most beautiful flowers that shall bloom in today's and tomorrow's gardens.

Our divine plan is to return to at-one-ment with the Father-Mother Creator, and at some point and time we shall all experience the inner tug that will pull us forward toward this great goal. The time will come when we shall cast aside the earthly shackles altogether, and as the flower opens to the sunlight, we shall unfold into the great spiritual evolution of perfection.

How beautiful the moment of ascension when the soul is freed from all the ties that have held it over its long past, and the awakened Christ consciousness, fully bloomed, ascends to the mountaintops of expression and from there, rises unfettered into the light and glory of God's kingdom come!

Longings of the Soul

Our soul longs for God. All of our desires represent the deep longing of our soul for oneness with God, our creative Source.

We long to know God in all His beautiful expressions—love, life, power, peace, beauty, companionship—and more. However, in most instances, we interpret this longing for God as a desire for things and things in themselves can never bring satisfaction. Satisfaction comes when we have a clear, vivid consciousness of the indwelling presence of God, our Father.

We are told in Matthew 6:33, *"Seek first his kingdom and his righteousness, and all these things shall be yours as well."*

It has been said that man's greatest mistake is in trying to become God, instead of simply being. This soul has been longing for something that is right within itself! We do not try to become, we simply be. How can we become that which we already are? We are a part of God and it is time we claimed this kinship definitely, *right now.*

Always know God within. Herein is the greatest blessing for all humanity. See the other fellow in the same way as you see yourself—see the radiant Christ in the face of every person you meet. This is our greatest privilege and the greatest training exercise we can perform. *See the radiant Christ in the face of every person you meet, every person you now know.* When you come to realize and accept the Christ, the God spark within each and every person, you will know we all are the same; we are one; made in His likeness always.

There is not one person who could not master every situation that arises, simply by knowing that God within gives him the complete power to be master of himself and of his life!

However earnestly you seek in the outer, you are

always unsatisfied and restless until you have a clear, vivid, consciousness of the indwelling presence of God, our Father. No matter how dear and near to you other persons may be, always you are searching for something deeper, which is the conscious companionship of God, so that God is no longer far removed from your everyday life, but a constant living part of your life. When you do reach the realization of God's indwelling presence, you have discovered one of the greatest secrets of the ages. You have also found the secret place of the Most High.

The Secret Place of the Most High

The secret place of the Most High is the mystical union between man and the Spirit of God. It is in the secret place that the awakening of our consciousness takes place, bringing illumination, quickening, revelation, inspiration, and realization.

The secret place of the Most High is the place where the soul becomes consciously aware of its sonship—or its divine birthright. It is God's own presence in you that belongs to you alone. It is the place where no one else can intrude.

An old Hindu proverb states: *"If God wished to hide, God would choose man to hide in."* It is apparent that this is the last place man usually thinks to look for God . . . within himself!

Humanity's problem today is that man is trying to become something that he already is. Man is trying to find something that is already within him. We are seeking and searching everywhere outside ourself for God, attending countless lectures, meetings, groups;

40

reading innumerable books; looking to teachers and personalities and leaders, when all the time God is within us. This is not to say that searching is not right. We are each impressed and guided in many different ways, but let us not become so absorbed in searching that we fail to *find* what we already have.

Jesus told us that the Truth would make us free. When you can stand in that free, flowing stream of universal power, nothing can touch you, let alone hinder or stop you. The almighty and all-pervading Father-Mother Principle joining with our own awakened consciousness forms a beautiful and effective secret place of the Most High which shines forth ever triumphant from within you to all the world, and it is the light, love, and beauty you shall always experience if you will only let Truth and light be your guide.

Where Are We Now?

Through eons of time, wrong thinking has allowed negative feelings such as fear, doubt, lack, weakness, and sickness to become embedded in man's consciousness to the extent that the reality of our true heritage as children of God has become clouded. The beautiful power of God flowing through us has often been infiltrated with wrong beliefs and actions, and man is a mere shadow of his true glory.

Instead of living in the knowledge of divine wholeness and divine oneness with God, we become beset with disease. Our constant supply dwindles to a mere trickle of its true abundant potential. Replacing the peaceful harmony of our brotherhood, we begin to dislike, find fault with, and even fight and kill one another. We begin to suffer in many ways, and it is all useless and unnecessary suffering. This has never been punishment from God, our Father, but results from causes we have set into motion.

We have forgotten that, as spiritual beings as well as physical beings, we have dominion and authority over our thoughts, feelings, and actions. So often we have used our blessed formative powers in wrong ways and based our thinking on the wrong use of our five senses.

Where Can We Be?

If we will direct our full attention to our loving Father and become centered in the light of God's consciousness within ourself, we will release all shackles that bind.

What is man that thou art mindful of him,
and the son of man that thou dost care for him?
Yet thou hast made him little less than God,
and dost crown him with glory and honor.
Thou hast given him dominion over the works of
    thy hands;
thou hast put all things under his feet,
all sheep and oxen,
and also the beasts of the field,
the birds of the air, and the fish of the sea,
whatever passes along the paths of the sea.
O LORD, our Lord,
How majestic is thy name in all the earth!
           —Psalms 8:4-9

It is up to you to claim your inheritance, for in order to realize the manifestation of your inheritance, you must first lay claim to it. You do this by right thinking, right feeling, and right action. You are a co-worker with God; He will work with you but not for you.

You should realize that you are the director for this good, and your elder brother Jesus clearly pointed the way. You should direct your thoughts, your emotions, and your actions toward daily living in harmony with the great universal laws. The good you give forth must then return to you as your own manifested good. Project right living and right thinking and you will receive abundant good health. Send forth love and peace, then the same must flow back into your own life and affairs.

Think on this affirmation: *I desire to be strong enough to be gentle and reap the rewards of the strong in Christ consciousness. I desire to live in the knowing that my own indwelling Christ is a powerful and effective connector to the Fountainhead of God, constant always, and eager to help me in every way.*

The instant you place your thoughts entirely on the divinity that is already established within you, dominion over every part of your life will be gained. You become in harmony with God and His good expresses through you.

Your relation to God is much like that of the sunbeam to the sun. Nothing can separate the sun from one of its rays. Made of the sun's substance, partaking of its nature, each sunbeam has a particular mission, a certain spot of the earth to caress and warm and light. Like the sunbeam, you too have your own special spot to fill, your own special work to do. Thus you are a vital part of the divine plan and necessary to the perfect whole.

An old Sufi legend beautifully depicts our journey through life and I would like to share it with you.

Long ago, in a far distant country, beautiful mountains stretched their peaks toward azure skies. High in these mountains a small spring bubbled from the rocks and trickled down the mountainside. It swirled around rocks, flowed smoothly under spreading trees, and gently kissed the banks that cradled it.

The stream was happy for it knew its destiny was to one day reach the great ocean and merge its waters with those of the sea. The stream flowed on its journey, passing through every kind and description of countryside—mountains, valleys, and plains. At last it reached the imposing sands of the great desert. Just as the stream had crossed every other barrier it had met, so too it tried to cross the great desert. But something happened. As fast as the stream flowed its waters onto the sands, the waters disappeared!

The stream tried again. The same thing happened. The dry sands thirstily absorbed the water. Now the stream was convinced that its destiny was to cross this desert and reach the sea, yet no way seemed possible.

Then from somewhere deep within the consciousness of the stream—or did it come from the desert?—a voice whispered, "The wind crosses the desert, and so can the stream."

"But how?" thought the stream. "I dash my waters

against the hot, dry sands, and they only become absorbed. The wind can fly, and this is how it crosses the desert. I cannot fly."

"But there is a way," again came the voice. "As long as you hurtle yourself against the sands in your old accustomed way, you cannot cross. You can only become a marsh, or disappear entirely. Let the wind carry you across to your destination."

"But how can this happen?" thought the stream. Never before had it been absorbed. What would the experience be like? Would the stream lose its identity? The idea wasn't too exciting. After all, the stream had its individuality and didn't want to lose what belonged to it. If it allowed itself to be absorbed by the wind, what assurance was there it would regain this individuality?

"Have no fear," came the voice. "Trust the wind. It will lift your waters high into the air, carry them across the vast desert, and let them gently fall to earth again. Your waters will fall as rain, and you can become a river."

The stream thought about this. A spark was kindled. "But how do I know this is true?" came the question.

"It is true. Have faith. If you do not believe, then you can never become more than a quagmire, and even that, my friend, could take a long, long time. Certainly a quagmire bears no relationship to a beautiful flowing river—or a stream."

That was heavy information. Then an idea came, "But why can't I remain the same stream I am today?"

"Because life is constant change. There is no way

you can remain exactly the same. Your waters must flow somewhere or progress in some way. You are a stream today because you do not yet realize that there is a greater, more essential part of you."

When the stream heard this, faint echoes of an eternal reality began to stir in his memory. Vaguely, he began to remember. Yes, it did seem as if there was a time when he had been gently held in the arms of the wind—or was it a dream? What was real? Clearly a decision had to be made. What must he do?

The stream thought for a while and made the decision. He raised his vapors into the welcoming arms of the wind. Oh, it was so easy! The wind gently and easily bore the vapors upward along the air currents, and after a while, let them fall gently as they reached the peak of a great mountain hundreds of miles across the desert.

Yes, now the stream remembered. Gently raindrops caressed the ground with life-giving water, and the stream continued on his journey toward the great ocean. Because of the experience, the stream more clearly remembered the truth of his being, for etched deeper into his consciousness were the details of growth. He reflected, "Thank You, Father, I have learned my true identity!"

The stream was learning, just as we are learning, day by day, more of our own importance and the Father's great caring for us. But the sands in the story whispered when they saw what happened, "We know, because we see it happen every day and because we, the sands, extend all the way from the stream's end to the mountains."

What you know in your heart determines what you

express. Do you believe that you are the child of a King? Do you believe you are truly a grand cosmic being? Are the faint whisperings that this is true beginning to stir in your soul?

Your Mission in Life

Like the stream in the story, your mission in life is to learn your true identity and to grow, step by beautiful step, in this knowledge and awareness toward total expression of your God-self. Your mission is that of awakening the sleeping Self within to all its infinite possibilities. *Awaken now to the reality of your divinity.* Realize and release the tremendous dynamo of power that is within you.

As a child of God, you have unlimited freedom. You even have the freedom to make mistakes. You have the freedom to seek answers to whatever questions dwell in your mind. You have the freedom to take your life in hand and magnificently solve your own problems.

You are going through the human experience of life on your way toward the magnificent, complete, and perfect expression of your true Self.

Abraham Lincoln once said, "I will study and get ready and the opportunity will come." You too can be ready for all life's opportunities, if you will study and prepare yourself. You never know when that special channel will open, but be ready. You can do this by constantly fanning the spark of your *divine potential* into a bright, beautiful, living, all-encompassing flame of Truth that burns out all that is unworthy and brings you into focus with the light, the

Creator, the divine Presence that is moving through you and through every other soul.

You are infinitely greater than you can conceive of being. Don't hide your light under a bushel, but stand upon a high mountain and let it shine out like a beacon everywhere. The light from one small candle is sufficient to dispel darkness. Be yourself at your highest and best; be yourself with the Christ light shining from within.

Be Yourself!

Don't let pressure conditions and circumstances squash you or obliterate you. Rise above the outer by turning on the inner light.

When we think of the ancient civilizations such as Rome and Greece, when we see all the wonderful things that man has built, the great scientific discoveries, we begin to catch a faint glimmer of what man can accomplish.

Take the time to have a daily talk with your Father God, and say something like this:

"Father, I do sincerely desire to become more attuned with Your life that flows through me. I bring the gift of my being, my awareness, to the altar of Truth. I offer myself, my talents, my abilities as a channel through which Your life can be expressed. I accept the challenge to improve any area of my life that needs to become better. Your life is seeing through my eyes, hearing through my ears, feeling through my touch, speaking through my lips, and loving through my heart. I am ready, Father, now. I am ready. I am completely ready to express, expe-

rience, reveal, and know the Truth of my being!"

Then quietly become still and know the presence of God. Be at peace with God and your labors and aspirations in all aspects of your life will keep peace with your soul. Be strong in character, for character faces up to life and rejects participation in anything less than absolute good from a fine moral discrimination and strength of will.

If God cradles the tiny sparrow in His loving, protecting, everlasting arms, will He not do likewise for you—His beloved child? Become receptive to the one Presence and the one Principle. Accept without delay the buoyancy of Spirit, soul, and body that God gives you. Release every difficulty and every decision to God. Leave the outworking to Him, the Source, for God will work with you and you have only to be silent, still, and receptive.

The loving Father always takes care of His children, and the divine love of our Father has one infallible sign: it works good in every way equally upon all. It does not rob one person to bless another, but in blessing one it blesses all.

Attitudes of Being

Your attitudes either help or hinder your participation in the Father's plan of good and abundance. Rise above the negative, restrictive attitudes that say, "No, I can't do it," and practice the attitudes that say, the Father and I are one and we can accomplish anything.

Since life is always an individual experience, and requires effort on your part, would you take some time each day for the next week and concentrate on the following be-attitudes? You will be richly blessed, and you will be able to stand as master of your own being and hold your course steadfast to the goal of receiving your Father's inheritance.

Alertness—I choose to be alert to the divine ideas that come to me. I open my mind and heart to the teaching of the spirit of Truth within, and accept my rightful heritage.

Willingness—I choose to be willing to grow, spiritually, mentally, and emotionally. All attitudes that are inadequate and unprofitable to my spiritual growth are eliminated as I let the transforming power of God perform its miracle-working changes in me.

Resourceful—I choose to use the mind my Father has provided to its greatest potential, and to learn and grow. With such a marvelous instrument as a clear, alert, and open mind, I am well equipped to handle any situation in life.

Powerful—I choose to exercise my God-given power to control my thoughts, feelings, and actions, inasmuch as my mind has the power to transform energy from one plane of consciousness to another. I will work to achieve peace, serenity, and success.

Love—I choose to allow my inner quality of love to see the good that is everywhere and in everybody. Love is the great harmonizer and healer and I will let pure, divine love adjust all misunderstandings and make my life and affairs healthy, happy, harmonious, and free.

Wisdom—I choose to place wisdom—the loving voice

of God within—as the source of understanding. This *intuitive knowing* transcends all intellectual knowledge. I let go of limited personal beliefs so that the Christ wisdom and divine understanding will shine through me.

Success—I choose to be successful in achieving my desired goals as a result of faithfulness and earnestness in the application of God's law in my life and affairs.

Go forth now, dear friend, and put into practice in your daily life the things you have learned. Living the law will open doors to all kinds of magnificent manifestations for you. With the wisdom of the Spirit of God as your guide, you will be led in all ways and realize your true identity as a beloved child of a King and a grand cosmic being.

Consciousness Conditioners

1. You are a child of the greatest King—God! Go forth each day and act in like manner.
2. You are important. There is a purpose for your embodiment in life.
3. Become attuned *with your own indwelling Christ Spirit.*
4. Simply *be!*
5. Become a constant dweller in your secret place of the Most High.
6. Life is constant change. You cannot remain exactly the same as you are right now.
7. Learn to become silent, still, and receptive to the wisdom of the Spirit of truth within you.
8. Practice daily the attitudes of Being.

9. See the radiant Christ in the face of every person you meet, and of every person you know.
10. Claim your rich inheritance now!

IV
Faith--God's Divine Gift

"Thy will be done in earth, as it is in
     Heaven."
Heaven's not a destination—
  It's a starting point.
  It's not a place in the sky
   where you and I
    are to spend an eternity
     in unprogressing bliss.
  Heaven's nothing like this.
For Heaven's the Kingdom of God within—
  The infinite life, love, joy, faith,
   wisdom, and strength of our divine
    self—
  The nature of God in us.
He who has discovered Heaven
  has not reached a destination,
   but a starting point
    for a new and wonderful life
     right here on earth!
           —J. Sig Paulson

The Cosmic Canvas

When an artist begins transferring an idea onto a new canvas, at first there may be only a baffling mixture of color and indistinguishable form. Then as the idea grows into more complete expression, the canvas begins to "live" with bright colors, intricate shadings, and the delicate brush strokes that add the finishing touch.

When an office building is in the construction stage, for a time a person passing by the construction site will see only the deeply laid foundation and the towering steel skeleton. There is no evidence of what the completed structure will look like. If we trace any idea or work from its beginning, we often find that at first it goes through a stage of formlessness, a period of seeming nothingness until a semblance of order is produced in outer form. Then the eye can discern what is happening.

The artist does have a definite design in his mind and it emerges in time as a beautiful and often inspiring picture on his canvas. The building contractor is also working according to a plan and it eventually becomes apparent. Often we can see periods of formlessness, times of seeming confusion, when ideas are in the embryonic stage and life may seem to be chaotic; but what once appeared chaotic progressively evolved into a beautiful outpicturing in life. How comforting is the awareness that we are ever evolving. God's infinite power is always working in perfect order and precision to bring mankind onward and upward in growth.

A lovely poem written by Russell A. Kemp says a

lot about what we are each painting on our own cosmic canvas of life. It is entitled "Precious Seed":

> *In what we live, in what we read,*
> *In what we share with another's need,*
> *In how we grow, to what aspire,*
> *In lifting our vision ever higher;*
> *In deeds of kindness and words of praise,*
> *In quiet hours and busy days,*
> *In little things that are great indeed,*
> *We sow the kingdom's precious seed.*

"We sow the kingdom's precious seed!" What an *alive* thought. What a magnificent divine blueprint can sprout from precious seed ideas. We are given so many precious seeds by our loving Father, and I believe the most important of these is faith. This precious seed of faith has been carefully planted within our being, but its growth must be diligently sought, carefully nourished, and patiently developed.

How does a tiny seed grow? Think about it for a moment. First, it is sown in the ground, and that ground can be dry, rocky, sandy, barren, or fertile. As the life force begins to move in the seed, it must first break through the protecting shell. As the life force becomes stronger, the seed germinates and works its way upward through numerous particles of earth before breaking through into the air. Then it must triumph over hot sunlight, drenching rains, and bending winds to grow into the strong, productive plant it has the capability of being.

The seed of faith is an attribute of God. Faith is purely and totally spiritual and knows only complete assurance. Faith is an ever-abiding awareness of God, a voice deep within each heart that says, *"I am here,*

beloved child, you are not alone. I am by your side.
Trust in Me for My love holds no limitations. My
ways are the perfect joining of wisdom and love
which bring right action and perfect peace!"

Faith is dauntless and cannot know defeat. It has
the insight to pierce through the confusion of that
which visible to know the strength and certainty of
the invisible. Once true faith is gained—the unshakable faith built on knowledge—it can never be
lost or taken away.

You may observe family, friends, neighbors, or
acquaintances who exhibit a faith as strong as the
Rock of Gibraltar; and you may think it is so easy for
them. But you can be assured that this strong, work-
able trust in God manifesting as faith *wasn't built
overnight.* The seed was carefully nurtured and
caressed into becoming the tender young belief, and
then tended into becoming the strong mature outpicturing of faith. Many years of study, awareness,
concerted prayer, and deep meditation may have
passed before this faith blossomed forth into full
flowering. And many lifetimes probably have tran-
spired to bring this faith to its current stage of
development.

Faith Now!

You don't have to wait to develop faith. That seed
within you is begging to be released and allowed to
grow. Let it!

Begin by having faith in yourself right now. You
are a child of God. You were created in the image of
the divine blueprint. Commit your whole self to *being*

that which you *are*.

In Genesis 1:27 we are told, *"So God created man in his own image, in the image of God he created him; male and female he created them."*

The foundation for faith in yourself is the truth that you are a child of God and, as such, you inherit the divine nature. When God created man in His own image, He also endowed man with a will of his own with which to mold his life. God also blessed man with a resourcefulness to meet and overcome any problems that life might offer. Faith provides strength and renewed energy to the will and stimulates it to action. Many of us seem able to manage situations in life quite well until some catastrophe strikes without warning; then we flounder and often feel unequipped to handle the situation.

At times like this, we may feel a deep need for something we didn't develop, something we didn't think about before, something that was right at hand all along but ignored because all was going well.

At that point, there is one important thing we can do. Turn to God for the answer. *Acquire and develop an unshakable faith in God.* How is this done? In Mark 11:24 we are told, *"Whatever you ask in prayer, believe that you receive it, and you will."*

What Is This Thing Called Faith?

A close analysis shows that faith is the foundation of all that man does. Faith is more than mere belief. It is the very substance of that which is believed. Faith works through love. Thoughts of condemnation, enmity, and resistance must be released and divine love declared; then faith can do its magnificent work unhindered. No life can be harmonious without faith and love abiding in the consciousness of the person.

Faith is the perceiving power of the mind linked with the power to shape substance. Spiritual assurance is the power to do the seemingly impossible. It is a magnetic power that draws unto us our heart's desire from the invisible spiritual substance. Faith is the deep inner knowing that what is sought is already ours for the taking.

Strong convictions and unwavering faith are the parents of all the great and enduring achievements of the human spirit. How many times have you had the strong desire to do something that your family and friends said couldn't be done, but somehow, deep within your being, you had the assurance that the task could be accomplished? So you dared to put forth the effort toward doing that which you desired and it worked. Your desire wasn't impossible to accomplish because you had the faith, the inner knowing it could be done; and it was yours for the taking because you put forth the necessary effort.

Inspired ideas quickly bloom into manifestation when placed in the rich soil of a faith-filled mind.

Faith is the real foundation of all that we do. Our conduct in life is governed by faith. Our reasoning faculty stops short at the boundaries of what is known, so from that point we must proceed to make progress by other means. We must step beyond the "known" and commit our whole self to that which God has done and is doing. The development of the faith faculty is a key to spiritual realization. *Faith, working in spiritual substance, accomplishes all things.*

This is the understanding faith that cooperates with creative law. When faith is exercised deep in a spiritual consciousness under divine law, without variation or disappointment, it brings results that are seemingly miraculous. Faith is related to the divine intuition or inspiration that comes to people at their best moments and gives meaning and coherence to their experiences. Actions backed by faith have overthrown kingdoms, quenched raging fires, stopped wars, and converted weakness into enduring strength.

Faith is the quality of the mind that moves and molds ideas and brings them into concrete expression. Faith is the perfect assurance and confidence of the mind that invisible substance is the Source of all visible material things.

Look around! All about you are inspiring examples of God's goodness and power working in the lives of His children. Tasty vegetables grow in a garden; fruit trees produce delicious and nourishing fruit; an injury is healed; and prayers are answered.

Faith in God, faith in self, and faith in all mankind compose a beautiful trinity. The greatest men have had faith in other men, and faith in their own inherent divinity. Through faith in our fellowmen we find God in manifestation.

As we use our faith, we develop more faith because the exercise of it has shown us what we can do.

Faith, like muscle, develops and increases in strength through use.

A little seed of faith exercised with understanding is mighty to remove obstacles that loom before us.

The engineer who moves a mountain of earth has first moved it in his mind by visualizing his ability to do so.

Five Minutes More

One of the most famous battles of history was fought at Waterloo when the English, under guidance of the Duke of Wellington, defeated the French, commanded by the so-called invincible Napoleon. Sometime later, Wellington was asked if the deciding factor of the battle was the bravery of the British soldiers. He replied, "British soldiers are no braver than French soldiers, but accomplished what they did because they were brave five minutes longer!"

So you can see that a matter of five minutes more may have changed the history of both France and England. The men had the faith to hang on, to keep fighting bravely, and they won the battle. Yet, how many of us relate this idea to ourself? How many of us stop to think that five minutes more spent in prayer, in having faith in God and in ourself may change an unwanted condition? Five minutes more of faith in ourself, and we may accomplish that seemingly "impossible" task. Five minutes more of believing and being patient and we may win the reward we are so earnestly seeking. Or the lack of that five minutes more of "hanging in there" could be our personal Waterloo. This is the meaning of the statement, "Keep on keeping on!" But we must remember that keeping on doesn't necessarily mean rushing on.

How Do You Cultivate Faith?

Everyone knowingly or unknowingly puts constant faith in the laws of nature. It has been said that mere walking is continual falling. You stand on one foot and throw yourself forward, relying on the force of gravity to bring your body into position to be caught by the other foot. Now if the force of gravity should change, becoming lesser or greater or reversed in direction, the result would be disastrous. So it is literally true that we all walk by faith—although it may be an unconscious faith in the law of gravity. We may not understand the physics involved, but that isn't necessary. The important thing is that we have faith that we can walk and we walk.

From studying the experiences of Peter, we can see the development of the faith faculty. The vacillating allegiance of Peter to Jesus illustrates the growth of faith in one whose faith faculty was not fully developed. Faith is built up through denial of all doubt and fear, and through continuous affirmation of loyalty to God's divine idea of perfection for you.

It is important to have faith in your spiritual capacity and to depend upon it in the face of any adverse appearances. Effort spent in pursuit of your ideal is delightful. You feel powerful and successful when your endeavors appear to be conquering difficulties. Since faith is a seed gift from omnipresent God, it transcends time and space and manifests in the eternal now.

Faith is not only a conviction that the unseen can become visible, it is also a definite movement toward rendering the idea tangible.

How Belief Becomes Faith

Often people become confused over the meanings of belief and faith. Both faculties are important. An inner acceptance of an idea as being true is belief, and belief can function both consciously and subconsciously. Belief is the child of divine power and will grow into faith when it is nurtured and fed, but it must be cultivated in order to grow.

Belief is the small child learning to walk, while faith is the child grown into a strong youth who can run a winning race.

Belief places all fulfillment and hope into the future. Faith establishes the absolute in the now. Belief depicts a desire in the act of becoming. Faith establishes the desire in present actuality. *Belief is necessary.* Hold on to it with determined tenacity, for belief, through use, will advance into the full-blown glory of faith. Faith matures into knowledge, and knowledge is the power and ability to create a better life.

Belief is like the ignition of a car, and faith is like the running motor. You must first turn the key in the ignition before the motor will start and run. Turning the key in the ignition is the necessary first step of right order.

Ralph Waldo Emerson defined belief when he said: *"All great ages have been ages of belief. I mean, when there was an extraordinary power of performance, when great national movements began, when the arts appeared, when heroes existed, when poems were made, the human soul was in earnest."*

Does the world run on faith or facts? In your purse

or pocket you have a handful of printed paper. You can go out and exchange this paper for many kinds of commodities, but only because people have faith that the government will continue backing up its paper money. You may have a checkbook, credit cards, and deeds to property. These are all articles of faith. They are affirmations of our belief that life will continue as it is now.

Understanding Faith and Blind Faith

Understanding faith is faith which functions from Principle. It is based on knowledge of Truth. It understands the law of mind action; therefore, it has great strength. To know that certain causes produce certain results gives a bedrock foundation for faith.

Blind faith is using faith without knowing or understanding what may be ahead. And that is good too! Blind faith is an instinctive trust in a power higher than ourself. However, as we learn and grow, we must grasp the principles of life beyond blind faith so we can direct our course instead of stumbling blindly forward. Blind faith has been referred to as a "state of unquestioning, blind acquiescence, involving no reason, no explanation, and no individual trait." Because blind faith does not understand the principles of Being and the vital life force, it is susceptible to discouragement and disappointment.

Practice Faith-Thinking

All of us have our thinking faculty located in the mind, from which we send forth all kinds of thoughts. If we are educated and molded after the average pattern of the human family, we may live a lifetime and never have an original thought. Our thinking faculty is supplied with second-hand ideas of our ancestors, dominant beliefs of the race consciousness, or threadbare thoughts of the ordinary social whirl. We often forget that the most important power of man is the original faith-thinking faculty, for this is the flowering of an enlightened mind.

Faith-thinking is accomplished when we catch sight of the Truth of our being and feed our thinking faculty on images generated in the faith center. Faith-thinking is not merely an intellectual process based on reasoning. The faith-thinker does not compare, analyze, or draw conclusions from known premises. He does not take appearances into consideration; he is not biased by precedent. His thinking gives form, without question, to ideas that come straight from the eternal fountain of wisdom—the God-Source. His perception impinges on the spiritual Truth and he simply knows.

Many times you may seem to be tested again and again that you might be strong in your faith, and sometimes it is necessary for you to let go of an avenue of thinking that you consider to be your dearest possession before you can realize divine providence. This law of giving and receiving pertains to the realm of ideas. You must let go of personal attachments to your thoughts before you can receive the greater inspiration from universal Mind. When you desire to refurbish the living quarters of your life, you must first be willing to part with the old, no longer useful, unwanted habits and belongings. In order to raise a new crop of ideas, it becomes necessary to root out the ineffective plantings of former years and make room for the new, the different, the more useful, more valuable harvest of the future. But you never have to do this alone.

Whatever happens in your world, your faith must not falter. Faith whispers deep inside your being that God is with you.

I often think of Helen Keller and the beautiful and meaningful words she spoke. *"Dark as my path may seem to others, I carry a magic light in my heart. Faith, the spiritual strong searchlight, illumines the way. Although sinister doubts lurk in the shadow, I walk unafraid toward the Enchanted Wood where the foliage is always green, and where life and death are one in the presence of the Lord."*

The Motivating Power of Faith

When you know what you want, you take intelligent steps to obtain your goal. What is the motivating power? Of course, you are moved by the vital life force itself. However, individually you are moved by the faith you have in your ideas according to the intensity of your desire. For desire is a power that moves, produces action, and engenders successful efforts, creating important effects.

One of the most striking characteristics you possess is your ability to know, to recognize, and to express your desires in conscious acts.

This particular trait effects great influence in the unfolding of human mind power. We have created environments, specified ways of life, and advanced our state of consciousness all through the action of desire prompted by faith.

Once you understand that your desire, the whispering of the "still, small voice," comes from God, the Source of all ideas, you begin to understand the meaning and value of faith toward the achievement of permanent good rather than temporary satisfaction. If you are trying to clear your mind of useless notions in order to fill this same reservoir with movement based on keen desire which will lead to definite action, the usual efforts are not good enough.

Faith laughs at seeming impossibilities and says, "It shall be done!" When Neil A. Armstrong, Edwin E. Aldrin, Jr., and Michael Collins, the first astronauts, launched their historical trip to the moon in 1969, they did not know what their fate would be, but their faith was adventurous.

You too must have the courage to "launch out," to take a gigantic step forward toward your goal—and toward a better life.

When you have the faith in God to let Him show you how to use the precious seed which is implanted within you, all your talents will increase and become a blessing to you and to others. This is the simplicity of faith by which your world can be remade and without which it is being un-made!

Faith Is an Important Tool

Faith linked with desire and imagination is your ability to carve the substance of life into such shapes as you may choose—consciously or unconsciously. As an instrument, faith is self-sharpening. It grows with use. Once you become aware of the power of your faith, you can connect every action you take with the use of that powerful tool. As you become conscious of your thoughts of faith in any enterprise, you know that if you were without faith in your life, you would make no further progress.

Man's basic instincts are protective. Our intuitions are helpful in many ways when we listen; but our vital inner powers are almost unknown. We seek food, shelter, warmth, and companionship because we are human, and these things are all good. We listen in amazement to those "whisperings of immortality" that have prompted many great souls to high thought, great effort, and immortal accomplishments. If we would right now begin to contemplate seriously the powers within ourself that we use only slightly, how vastly better our life would become.

We have the power of sight and use it to gaze at distant stars, scrutinize microscopic life, and enjoy the scene before us. We have the power of speech and some use it to become great orators or prolific writers. We have the power of movement and use it to transport us to places all over the earth, plunging into depths of the oceans and soaring to great heights in the air. But when we thoroughly awaken to our great inner powers and to the new energies we can control within ourself, we become new persons, vitally alive, and we reach unheard of achievements.

To cut bread, one secures the loaf and a knife. *To live life, you discover an objective, and apply energy!* Like any other instrument, faith will work where it is applied; if not applied, there will be no work.

The world answers us back according to our faith.

It trusts when we trust. It responds magnetically to our confidence. It says to the farmer, "sow your seeds," and new plants grow. It says to the aviator, "spread your wings," and huge jets fly around the world. It says to the individual, "follow that dream!" and man voyages to the moon.

Action Steps

Today you have twenty-four wonderful, unused, potential-packed hours. What are you going to do with them?

Today is the perfect moment in your life to take the time to analyze what you are doing and where you are going. Put out of your mind all thoughts of doubt, worry, or uncertainty of how situations in life can be solved. Clear the way so your faith can become active as you work with God in your thoughts, words, and actions.

Faith is strengthened by rejoicing in thoughts of God's abundance. Start giving thanks for the abundance that God already has prepared for you in spiritual substance. By working lovingly and joyfully with God, you make it possible for His energy to work through all the conditions and persons in your life.

Place your faith in the positive ideas of good rather than in the seemingly negative ideas of the world. You are given the power to create conditions in your life through your thoughts, words, and actions. Often false conditions are created that are not true reality. These false conditions manifest as fear, hate, selfishness, suspicion, and *none of these is in harmony with God's good creations.* But when you have enough faith to live in God's kingdom of creations, the kingdom of perfection, you will prosper and find only success.

For a period of one week, think about faith and use the following faith affirmations to change your life. Take seven opportunity-packed days and work with the idea of cultivating the precious seed of faith so your divine blueprint can unfold in its greatest manifestation.

1. I believe in the presence and power of God, and my faith grows greater day by day.

2. I have the faith to allow God's loving will to be manifested through me in all my affairs.

3. I have faith in God's omnipresent supply and know my needs are abundantly met.

4. I have faith to lift my voice in prayer. God's perfect healing power removes all doubts and fears from my mind.

5. I have faith in God. I relax and enjoy each new life experience, knowing that any problem situations have a beautiful and perfect solution.

6. I have the faith to let God show me the right avenue to follow, and my divine blueprint unfolds perfectly.

7. I have faith that faith works! I express my desires in conscious acts.

Consciousness Conditioners

1. You are painting your own cosmic canvas of life. How will the picture unfold?
2. The seed of faith is an attribute of God given to you—freely and lovingly.
3. *Faith is dauntless* and cannot know defeat.
4. Once true faith is gained—the unshakable faith built upon knowledge—it can never be lost or taken away.
5. You don't have to wait to develop faith. That seed within you is begging to be released and allowed to grow.
6. Commit your whole self to *being* that which you *are.*
7. Inspired ideas quickly bloom into manifestation when placed in the rich soil of a faith-filled mind.
8. Faith, like muscle, develops and increases in strength through use.
9. Practice *faith-thinking.*
10. Put your inspired desire into action, for *desire is a power that moves, produces action, and engenders successful efforts, creating important effects.*

V

Mind: Your Master Power

Attunement

There is always something beautiful to be found if you will look for it. Concentrate your thoughts on the good, beautiful, and true things of life rather than the reverse. This positive, loving attitude of mind towards life and people will help you to perceive the presence of God active in your life, helping you to wonderfully utilize your vital life force and put into operation the divine magic that opens all doors.

Thought

Thought—the act or process of thinking—is one of the greatest powers we possess and like most powers, it can be used positively or negatively, as we choose. The great majority of people have never been taught how to use thought, the master power of the mind. It is just as essential to know how to think correctly as it is to know how to speak or act correctly. The mind is kept active through thought.

Thought is necessary for the mind to remain strong

and powerful. The mind must be kept in use, otherwise it becomes stagnant and dormant. Remember that thought and mind are abstract, yet practically all of their manifestations are of a concrete nature. Thought is produced by the subconscious and superconscious phases of the mind, and is not a product of the intellect.

How Thoughts Are Formed from Mental Energy

Many people find it hard to understand the tremendous power manifesting in ordinary thought, yet they can easily understand the power generated by steam or electricity. They can see these forces at work and understand their functions, whereas thought power is vague and not always easy to comprehend.

Thought power is present in two avenues of operation: direct and indirect.

The indirect action of thought is easy to understand, for obviously a person must think before he can do anything. Thought is the motivating power behind an action, just as electricity is the motivating power behind lighting our home. *Thought also has a direct action on matter.* Regardless of whether or not we translate our thought into actual performance, the thought itself has already produced some kind of effect.

There are many kinds of matter, and some of them are so fine we cannot see them with our limited physical sight, but the vibrations from a person's thoughts can act directly upon particles of matter and set them in motion. When thought vibration produced within the mental body of a person is communicated to external matter, an effect is produced. Now it is easy to understand how and why thought itself is a very real and definite power; and every living, breathing one of us possesses this power.

Thought is no respecter of persons. Everyone, rich and poor, young and old alike, holds the power of thought in his mind. The important thing is to learn to use this tremendous power beneficially.

Let the forces of habit within you become positive. When you accustom your mental body to certain types of vibrations, your mind learns to reproduce these vibrations quickly and easily. If you allow yourself to think in a particular manner today, it will be easier to think in that same manner tomorrow. This is how you often do unconscious harm to yourself and to others with your thoughts, and this is the way ridiculous prejudices arise that blind you to the good attributes of a person or a situation.

Ancient Truth: Like Attracts Like

The philosophy of like attracting like also applies to thinking. Try this experiment:

Close your eyes and imagine thousands of tiny thought particles moving around in space. Each one is glowing with a bright light which seems to come from its very center. Each thought particle is trembling violently with its vibrations and moving like a comet through space. Some of them are going north and south, some are moving east and west, some are moving up or down, and others are traveling in various diagonal directions.

Occasionally two of these tiny thought particles bump together and, never stopping, stick together and continue in the orbit of the strongest vibration. They unite their vibration, tremble in unison, and continue to move on. These two thought particles may meet a third and fourth thought particle and, joining with them into one larger trembling unit, they move on until many thought particles might be gathered together. Some other thought particles that come close to this unit may tag along or they may jump away, repulsed. It all depends on what type of vibration the master unit consists of.

A strong reaction is produced upon the thinker by the thoughts he generates.

If your thought is directed toward someone else, it flies like a well-directed missile toward that person. If your thought is connected mostly with yourself, it remains close, floating in the ethers nearby, just waiting for an opportunity to react upon you and reproduce itself. This sometimes causes you to feel as though a thought simply popped into your mind from nowhere, but the experience is really the mechanical result of your own previous thought.

How Your Thoughts Affect Others

You should understand this amazing power of thought and strive to transmute any unconstructive, unkind, or selfish thoughts. Whether you wish it or not, thoughts *will* produce their effect and each time you try to control your thoughts, control becomes a little easier.

Sending out a good thought to another person is

just as real as giving that person a large sum of money or an expensive gift. This is a form of giving that is possible for everyone.

A wise person strives to produce results intentionally. To radiate negative thoughts is wrong and harmful. It causes undue suffering to sensitive people as well as to the creator of these thoughts, and it also prevents higher thoughts from coming in to the sender. Our thoughts are not our own business conclusively, for the vibrations we emit must affect others as well as ourself, and a negative thought can travel as far as an ill-spoken word.

How to Stimulate Your Thought Center

When forming your mental creation, you must realize this is a spiritual and scientific process that will *never fail to work* for you, if all the elements are properly provided. If it doesn't work and you don't receive the desired results, then one or more necessary elements were missing, or else the process was incorrectly performed.

Let us use the example of baking a cake. You must have the prescribed amounts of flour, milk, eggs, butter, flavoring, and all the other ingredients called for in the recipe to create a good cake. You have all the ingredients before you, so you prepare the batter according to the directions, then slide the cake into the oven which has been pre-heated to the desired temperature. The cake is allowed to bake a specific length of time. You remove your masterpiece from the oven when the timer alerts you . . . and it'   !
What happened?

Perhaps you used one too many eggs or not quite enough milk. The oven could have been too hot or not hot enough. Perhaps you should have baked the cake five minutes longer according to your altitude above sea level.

So you see, just as knowledge and skill combined with good ingredients are necessary to bake a cake, the same process applies to obtaining what you want from life.

One very important ingredient used to stimulate your thought center is the process of visualization. All of us use the power of visualization many times each day. Perhaps some of us are, for one reason or another, more thorough than others. Think about how a good architect goes about his work.

Before he ever picks up his pencil and ruler to begin planning a house or building, he must first see the completed structure in his mind's eye. He knows exactly where the circular staircase will be located and he knows where he is going to place the covered patio and the sunken living room, or he knows the specifications of where and how each office is to be constructed. Every closet, every door, every detail of the building design is in his mind's visualization well in advance of the first step in preparing the blueprint.

Now, this architect did not acquire his vast storehouse of knowledge overnight and neither will you acquire complete control over your thought center "muscles" immediately. They require a certain period for growth. For some of you, this apprentice time may be less, for others, more. But the great reward is the knowledge that *you can develop your thought center.* You can learn to obtain what you want from life. The first step is to learn how to ascertain your true desires and then maintain the persistence to work toward your goal until you get results.

The Importance of Right Use

Please keep in mind a vital word of caution when working with mind energy. Don't misuse it. You cannot use spiritual energy in a negative manner without reaping the consequences—and all energy is spiritual.

When you perform the act of thinking, you are using God power, for thinking is the connecting link between God and man. God expresses Himself to man through the golden glimmer of divine ideas. From these ideas we form mental images or pictures in our mind, based upon our acquired understanding, which images are often brought forth as actions and desires.

You are solely responsible for your thoughts. Each one of us is an individual soul personality with the opportunity to express free will. We are not puppets. Each of us has this free will and can choose for himself a particular path to follow. However, we all have consciousness in the one mind—the Divine Mind—the universal Mind. It is how each one *controls* his consciousness through thinking, feeling, and actions that gives the appearance of many minds.

Because God is the epitome of free will, *what was created in His image must also be given free will* and the opportunity to choose between an unlimited expression of good and a limited expression of good. Because God is the ultimate personification of life, truth, and love, His manifestation must also personify these attributes. You are this manifestation.

Man, through the gift of free will, is given the opportunity to master his consciousness by entering into the mastery of achieving the Christ consciousness, by *totally attuning his mind with the Mind of God.*

A lily sprouts, buds, blooms, and returns to the soil of the earth a lily still. Yet, a man can be born in seeming poverty and unenlightenment, but through mastering and controlling his destiny by his right thinking, he can rise as the sublime master over all limitations; and at the end of his incarnation, he can make the transition as a more spiritually-evolved soul. And isn't this beautiful Truth worth the effort to use rightly the wonderful power of mind?

How to Combat Negativity

Negativity blocks our contact with universal forces that are above human mind power. It is like using a block of wood to prevent two high-powered magnets from drawing together. An ancient mystic principle states that we must become aware of negativity *before* it can be destroyed or transmuted. It is impossible for you to break free from any harmful state or condition if you are unaware of its existence.

Any person who has ever experienced a business failure, a serious illness, rejection from a loved one, or any other shock or crisis has met negativity head on. Yet this very negativity we dislike so much is trying to give us a valuable tip: something within is not right.

People cling to negative states for many reasons.

Some get a strange sort of pleasure out of being negative, but why not remove the weeds from the garden and let the lovely flowers achieve their true growth and beauty?

Give up the negative feelings and find healthy pleasure in spiritual maturity.

A friend in one of my classes asked, "My main negative emotion is depression. What causes it and how can I cure it?" *Depression occurs when you catch a sudden insight into the looming emptiness of your life.* A woman may be caught up in the social whirl of playing bridge everyday, or a man may think he is sitting on top of the world with all his business achievements. Then they may catch a quick peek at their inner self and realize they are putting on an act. It is a little like dreaming of a shining castle and waking up inside a thatched hut! That is when depression sets in.

The cure is so simple. Be willing to see through your pretensions of leading a "purposeful" life. *Your true purpose comes from within.* When you have eliminated all illusions of the false self, the true purpose of being enters your life.

No, there is nothing at all wrong with being a successful businessman or with playing bridge with your friends. Be as outwardly prosperous as you desire, knowing that it won't add one thing to your inner life. A rich, effective inner life guarantees a prosperous and rewarding way of life. All right; this sounds terrific, but how do you eliminate negativity that is coming at you from another person? It is true that you cannot control another person, nor should you want to. But you can control the negativity that is flowing toward you from another person so it will not impinge upon you. *Reject these negative thoughts by denying their power to influence you.*

When you feel little darts of unpleasantness, pause, take a deep breath, and say, *"I do not wish to receive or accept any negative thoughts or feelings. Leave me at once and be transmuted into positive light!"* Then lift your head high and continue with whatever you are doing, in complete confidence that no negative thought can ever touch you without your acceptance of it.

How to Create Thought Forms

A thought form, any thought form, has its beginning within your mind. And just what is a thought form? It is any constructed thought about any person, place, or situation. Whether you originated the thought or someone else planted the seed, the beginning is mental. If your thought desire really means something to you, then you are going to add emotional energy to it. Always when building thought forms, remember to give them both mental and feeling energy. This combined effort is what gives life energy and reality.

A thought form is a congealed field of energy and has definite boundaries. The more definite you can make these boundaries, the more real your thought form becomes. Build in all the intricate details of your thought form. Build in the richness of color. Give your thought form the intensity of outline, the contrast of light and dark shadings. Give it intensity of feeling. Let yourself become a creator!

Start from scratch and build your thought form one little molecule at a time if necessary. You must be able to feel it and see it, out there in front of you. Make your thought form real! This is the key to its success.

When you build this much reality into your thought form, then release it to the cosmic universe with love, *nothing can stop it!* Automatically and methodically, in adherence to the law of cause and effect, it will gather unto itself whatever it needs to manifest.

Building thought forms is a very real technique and it is the basis upon which successful metaphysical treatment works.

Here's a good example of how a thought form works:

It has often been demonstrated with two tuning forks of the same pitch, that when one is struck, the other fork which is in close proximity, will vibrate in sympathy with the first. Since a thought form is vibrating energy and is emitting impulses of a particular frequency, it can cause a vibration in its counterpart in the material world. Thus, it establishes a rapport or a condition of attunement. Because of this attunement, one unit can affect the other and excite it or cause changes to be made in its manifestation to draw an individual to the object of his desires.

So you see, creating thought forms is no secret. Everyone has this ability. The important point is to learn to *create such a strong visual picture in your mind that the image of good you create will have to manifest itself as an object or an event on this physical plane of life.*

Before putting this process into practice, you must understand the important requirements involved. First, know exactly and clearly what specific thing you desire to manifest. You cannot concentrate on a dozen things at one time. Analyze carefully which important desire will *bring you* the most good and success and happiness in your life. You can work on other desires, one at a time, later.

Clear your mind of all obstacles. Most people's minds are cluttered up with a hodge-podge of thoughts of little or no consequence. Get rid of them! Hold one dominant thought in front of your mind. Visualize that one important thing you want. Now you are ready to begin your visualization process.

The Visualization Technique

I find it best to retreat to my private sanctum for this purpose. You will need to be in a place where you will not be distracted by a jangling telephone or by someone interrupting you right in the middle of your thought process. Settle comfortably in a nice easy chair and relax.

Begin with the tips of your toes. Direct all your thoughts toward helping those toes relax. Relax them one at a time, beginning with the big toe on your right foot, then relax the other four toes one at a time. Repeat this same process with the left foot.

Gradually work upwards in your relaxation process. Relax your ankles, the calves of your legs, your knees, and move slowly and gently upward until you reach the top of your head. Feel the tiny muscles in your face, around your eyes and ears, in your scalp, slowly and gently relax. This will take about five or six minutes and when accomplished, you will feel quieter and rested.

Now, direct your attention totally to your mind. The biggest problem with the average person is to slow down and stop the rapid flow of thoughts darting through his mind. When I started working with this process, I would feel I was taking great strides forward toward slowing down my mind. Then, just as I was completely relaxed and my mind was blank, the thought would occur that I had forgotten to add milk to the grocery list, or some equally distracting gremlin. But by continued efforts, I finally conquered unwanted thoughts, just as you will.

In your mind's eye, visualize the center of your forehead as being a giant screen. See this screen fill the entire space before you and visualize it as brilliantly lighted, just as a movie screen is sometimes illuminated before the film starts. Now, very carefully and slowly, begin to assemble on this screen of your conscious mind a *bold, living, and completely detailed picture* of what you wish to make manifest. Make it real! Be an artist! Even if you can't paint a flower physically, you can be a Rembrandt mentally. Fill in all the colors, bright and happy and good. If a smell is involved, make your visualization so real you can smell the aroma. Make it so real you can feel the touch, as of fabric, metal, or glass. Let your visualization live.

Hold that completed visualization firmly in your mind for two or three minutes. In doing this, you are literally creating that same situation in fact. Remember what I said about thought forms and vibrations? *You are now sending out a powerful vibration of the manifestation you wish.* The more sharply you can bring your visualization into focus, the more surely there will be a sympathetic attunement with the corresponding object of your imagery.

Now, end your period of visualization by wrapping your image in bountiful love and releasing it to the cosmic universe with the statement, "This, Father, or something better." Know that what is right and good for you will manifest, then forget about the desire. Don't permit your thoughts to turn back to what you have done for one instant. Don't permit any faint images of the visualization you have constructed to trail into your imagination. Put it completely out of your mind for now. This is very important for if you retain any portion of your visualization, you are siphoning off the vital energy which is necessary to its ultimate manifestation.

A simple manifestation may result from a single creative meditation period, whereas a large project may require several sessions. But it will work for you.

The laws of physics apply here just as they do everywhere in the universe. Once you have started the cosmic energy working for you by repeated visualizations of your desired objective, *make every physical effort to bring it about.* Don't sit back with the attitude, "Well, let's see if this thing really works." Believe it will work and do what you can to help it happen. Open the avenue of all possibilities. Isn't it much easier to walk through an open door than one which is closed? The manifestation of your desire may be waiting for you on the other side of the door, but you must turn the doorknob and push.

The best things in life are yours to have, not at the expense of others, but through your harmonious cooperation with the cosmic universe. However, here I want to emphasize two cardinal rules for obtaining life's desires:

1. Whatever the object of your desire, it must be good for all and cause no harm.

2. The object of your desire must not be coveted from another. Life holds more than enough substance for each of us to have an abundance in life without taking anything away from another.

Accept a word of advice here, please. Never plan recklessly, nor try to use the cosmic universe as a playground. You are working with forces and energies which are strong and when you break the laws, remember that a cosmic slap in the face can smart.

Consciousness Conditioners

1. Every material manifestation had its beginning as a thought.
2. Thought—the act or process of thinking—is one of the greatest powers you possess and, like almost all powers, it can be used positively or negatively as you choose.
3. Stop wasting energy in negative thinking. As you remove human negativity, your contact with universal spiritual power grows stronger.
4. There is not one single, painful mood that you cannot separate from your life.
5. Thought power is present in two avenues of operation—direct and indirect.

6. Ancient truth: like attracts like!
7. Create *vivid* thought forms. Let them grow into mental manifestation, then release them to the cosmic universe in loving expectation.
8. Make every *physical* effort to bring about your desire in addition to building a strong thought form.
9. Never plan recklessly, nor try to use the cosmic universe as a playground. Always say, "This or something better, Father."
10. Become a creator in the truest sense!

VI

Developing the Answer Attitude

Attunement

"There is within us a power that could lift the world out of its ignorance and misery if we only knew how to use it, if we would seek and find. When you meditate open not only your listening mind, but the other door of your mind as well, so that the spirit streams out as fast as it comes in. Store nothing. . . . A tree grows not by the pulling of the sun only, but by the richness of the soil. . . . Go into the calm and luminous silence to renew, but stay in the soil of your life. No, there is nothing to fear. Do not waste time wishing for peace; there is no peace in a world, there is only peace in one's own soul. Get more fearless peace into your souls and then you will be some good!"—*J. P. M.*,
        Letters of the Scattered Brotherhood

The Answer Attitude

We have considered the thinking process and

analyzed its effects in our life and affairs. Now, how do you develop the *answer attitude*—the attitude of mind that makes you master of life instead of slave, the attitude that brings the inner calmness and patience you desire instead of screaming tension and chronic anxiety, the attitude that is permanent and effective instead of fleeting and haphazard?

The direct road to obtaining the *answer attitude* is found through constantly turning your thoughts toward the spiritual aspects of life and letting them dwell on the infinite good in yourself and in others.

Use positive words and positive thoughts in everything you do. There is nothing but the perfect condition, the perfect outpicturing desired. Plant within your soul the perfect seed idea. Ask to manifest only the outworkings of this perfect seed idea—to manifest perfect health, to express perfect harmony, and to realize perfect abundance—not to be delivered from inharmony, misery, and limitations. Throw these attitudes off as you would discard an undesirable garment. They are old and outgrown attitudes and you can afford to discard them joyfully. Do not even turn to gaze upon them. They are forgiven and forgotten. They have returned to the substance from which they were created—transmuted and blessed.

Fill the seeming blank spaces about you with the thought of God, infinite good. Then remember the Word of God is a seed. It must grow. Leave the how, when, and where to the divine intelligence of the universe. Your route is to say what you want and to give forth blessings, knowing that the moment you have appropriately asked, you have received. *Ask! Affirm! Look to God for your spiritual attainment;*

then receive God's bounteous fulfillment.

You do not have to beseech God for your desires anymore than you have to beseech the sun to shine. The sun shines because it is a law of its very being to shine. God pours out His unlimited wisdom, love, supply, life, and abundance to you because to give is a law of His Being.

The only thing that can limit the fulfillment of your desires is your own lack of understanding and failure to go forward in Truth.

Now, you have learned about thought forms and you want to use your knowledge of building them by breathing life into them and sending them out to do good for you. A major consideration when working with thought forms is that if they are receptive and can do their work, they will. But if the thought form is improperly constructed and perhaps not for your highest good, then it comes rushing back to you. After all, you created it and it knows no other home. Thus you must understand that when you are sending out a thought form, there is a fifty-fifty chance (during your neophyte period) that it can come back to you. What kind of roulette do you want to play?

Let's work on some answer-attitude thought procedures for attracting personal benefits to you.

The Art of Healthy Thinking

The principal cause of illness lies in the fact that the average person continually and repeatedly abuses his body. Yet, our amazing automatic repair system operates so efficiently that we often repeat a serious and damaging abuse for years before it forces us to face the unhappy consequences of a breakdown in our body.

Doctors have an important place in the healing picture and you should never hesitate to consult your physician when the need arises. Sometimes a condition becomes so urgent that calling your physician is imperative so immediate application can be made of his medical knowledge. What you want to develop is the answer attitude of awareness and understanding that will eliminate abuse of your wonderful body.

The World's Greatest Healer

The greatest healer in the world is the golden elixir of the vital life force—spiritual energy.

This is the energy that creates and sustains life. It has been said that all disease is the result of an insufficient supply of spiritual energy. *The true art of healing consists of directing this energy to and through your body so that it flows through all the organs and parts which constitute the physical form.* These may sound like simple words, and they are! But you must learn certain universal truths which only become known and acquired by *practice*.

Any condition of an illness which manifests in your body is a result of something which has gone before that is not in harmony with universal law or principle.

The cause could come from many areas. The answer attitude is to change the inharmony into harmony, and the only limitation to healing energy is your own belief and expectation. The challenge is yours, don't let it go unheeded.

Forgiveness Heals

If any part of your mind, body, or affairs is experiencing a state of ill-health, there is something, someone, or some memory you need to freely forgive and release from your feelings forever. You may not even be consciously aware of what it is, but your subconscious mind—the storehouse of your emotions, feelings, and memories—knows what it is.

If you think someone has been unfair or unjust in dealing with you, you need to forgive. If you react with hurt feelings to something that has been said or implied, you *need* to forgive. If you feel someone has robbed you of a special happiness you felt was yours, you need to forgive. Forgive others and forgive yourself. Give up all false ideas of injustice and release all feelings of hurt, injury, and wounded pride.

It is through forgiveness that true spiritual healing is accomplished.

Forgiveness removes the errors of the mind, and bodily harmony results in agreement with divine law. The control of error thinking leads to the knowledge of the real Self, and knowledge of the real Self—the Spirit of truth in you—leads to greater control of consciousness. Such control must necessarily involve the discipline of the senses, mind, and heart as well as the harnessing of spiritual energy.

Forgiveness is blessing instead of blaming.

Forgiveness is releasing all feelings of retaliation.

Forgiveness is restoring a relationship to a friendly and loving condition.

As you live in the answer attitude of forgiveness, love, and peace, you become free with the freedom of

Spirit and you are healed.

Feel Supremely Happy

Three simple words have such magical properties for developing an answer attitude. *Feel supremely happy!* When you let yourself feel supremely happy, your whole body changes. Your thoughts, your facial expressions, your health, your attitudes, in fact, everything about you changes for the better. You have achieved the same state of mind as does the mystic when he contacts universal power. When you persist with this feeling and attitude until it becomes a vital part of your life, you can perform miracles with it. You will be in harmonious communion with the universe, all because you are thinking and believing and knowing the power of thought energy behind these three little words. Your body will respond to them miraculously.

Turning On Love

Human beings were not made to endure isolation from other members of the race, *nor were they made to endure loneliness.*

The ambition to do well, whether it is to culminate a big business contract or to prepare a delicious meal for a beloved family, is empty and hollow if it has selfish motive.

Everyone has a perfectly natural need for loving companionship and you can assert the fulfillment of that need through the answer attitude of love.

Love is the power that joins and binds the universe

and everything in it in divine harmony. It is the great harmonizing principle known to man. *There are two kinds of love—personal and impersonal.*

Love, on the impersonal level, is the ability to get along with other people. It is a constant feeling of goodwill directed to others without personal attachment. Divine love is impersonal. It loves for the sake of loving and makes no demands on the loved. Like the sun, its joy is in the shining forth of its nature.

Love is an inner quality that sees the good everywhere, in everything, in everybody. It insists that everything created by God is good, and it refuses to see less than omnipresent good and finally causes that good to transpire. Divine love will bring your own to you. It will help adjust all misunderstandings. It will make your life healthy, harmonious, happy, and free.

Personal love is the warmth of expressing the tenderness, kindness, devotion, appreciation, and caring that you feel for those in your family and circle of close friends. It is the expression of sharing deep and tender feelings with the person you love most in all the world.

If that special person is not currently in your life, remember the thought forms. Use this technique to help bring your rightful good into manifestation.

Prosperity—Your Divine Heritage

Begin right now to eliminate any thoughts that prosperity is something separate from your spiritual life. You are going to have a whole chapter showing you how to have more prosperity in your life. But for the moment, let us look at three basic elements you can use to earn the help of the cosmic universe to obtain ever-increasing prosperity.

A. Positive attitude

B. Vigorous action

C. Proper timing

Let's analyze these three elements, one at a time, and we will use obtaining more money as an example.

A. Positive attitude: This is a basic fundamental to any kind of growth. Embed firmly within your mind the reality that you can have more money. If there is one ounce of doubt that it is possible for you to have more money, you have not taken the first and most important step.

Our modern society realizes it is good for a person to accumulate enough wealth to build a business that brings employment and worthwhile services to the community. It is good to build a "nest egg" to provide your children with a well-rounded education, to purchase a desirable home, to provide for retirement, or for whatever purpose brings you growth, happiness, and comfort.

Never be covetous of another person's material wealth. Rejoice in his prosperity and rejoice in the realization that you too can have all the abundance you desire. It is one of the best ways to assure your own.

B. Vigorous action: This element can be a "stumbling block" for some people. Don't sit around waiting for your bundle of wealth to be dropped ceremoniously into your waiting lap, and with no effort on your part. Do what you can now. Make a self-supporting start on the basis of service. *Action is the indispensable element of success.*

Action includes some form of sharing what you have with others. Remember that what you give out must return to you many-fold. Give your share of God's energy to worthwhile causes, and you establish psychological and spiritual streams of prosperity. You become a magnet for prosperity. Be grateful. An attitude of gratitude is a powerful magnetizer. Think how completely dependent your ability to earn material wealth is on maintaining physical health.

C. Proper timing: Knowing the proper time to take action brings you right back to the area of expanding your spiritual perception. A good sense of timing is a function of that deeper aspect of life we call *awareness*. All of us have a little voice deep within that prompts us to go forward vigorously, then at other times it whispers to hold back until the right opportunity is available. It is very important to develop constant rapport with your inner voice. A good exercise to develop this attunement is to promise yourself that you will devote a certain amount of time during each day to listening to this guiding voice within and around you.

Spiritual growth is something you can only feel for yourself. No number of words ever written can take the place of your own personal mystical experiences which occur on the path to spiritual growth. Many times the first experience in spiritual growth is spontaneous when it comes and is often quite a surprise to its recipient. I'll share the experience of a friend with you. A portion of her letter is as follows:

"For some unknown reason, I awakened in the early hours of the morning. My mind was sort of fuzzy at first, then I became aware of a bar of beautiful blue light reaching across my bed. As I stared at this unusual sight, the bar began to expand and a door appeared at about the mid-point of the bar. I had the impression of sparkling colors whirling in an immense sky from the other side of the door, and I wanted to walk through the door and explore the beautiful world I sensed to be on the other side of the door.

"I must have fallen asleep again, for my bedside alarm awakened me at seven o'clock. I remembered my 'vision' or 'dream' of the previous night, but it had neither excited nor scared me. It feels good, and today I feel very close to God—as if some special attunement had occurred."

Let's continue with a program of planned spiritual growth for you. By now you should be fully aware that you are spirit. God is Spirit and you are a part of God. Begin each day by reaching inside yourself to touch the infinity which is the Spirit of God.

The following affirmations are special consciousness conditioners. Repeat them often during the day and drive their special message firmly into your subconscious mind.

Morning Affirmation

Divine Father, as I travel along the journey of life, let me this day control and direct the energies of my mind.

Afternoon Affirmation

Divine Father, let me this day hold the

positive answer attitude, bringing no nega-
tivity to another and becoming more
purified within myself.

Evening Affirmation

Divine Father, I am grateful for all the
opportunities which have blessed my life
this day. As my body relaxes in sleep, let
my mind assimilate all the good accrued
today, making it a part of my ever-expand-
ing consciousness.

The Regenerative Power of Denial and Affirmation

As you grow in spiritual awareness, you become aware of two fantastically effective processes—denial and affirmation. What is the meaning of denial? What happens to all inharmonious conditions when you use the power of denial? To "deny" means to withhold from, such as to withhold food from the hungry. Another meaning is to declare something to be untrue, or to repudiate it as utterly false.

If you are feeling filled with undesirable thoughts or manifestations in your life, denials will help you cleanse away all unwanted conditions and help make room for new blessings. Whatever good is needed to add new dimension to your life can be obtained by making your denial of unwanted conditions and affirming the positive or desired.

Denial is the mental process of cleansing and erasing from your consciousness all false beliefs of the sense mind.

A denial is a relinquishment and it should be made in loving understanding, not vehemently. Make your denial of a situation or circumstance gently and make your affirmations in a strong, bold, positive attitude.

Use denial to release any negative thoughts and conditions. Then when the vessel of your mind has been emptied of all unwanted elements, refill it abundantly by using positive affirmations to bring in complete good. Example:

Denial: *I empty myself of all that would keep me from positive thought and perfect loving action.*

Affirmation: *This day I will let God's divine will and love be fully in charge of my life and affairs and fill my being with complete good.*

With continued use of cleansing denials, the inharmonious conditions lose their power to make you unhappy. A vacuum is formed, enabling your positive affirmations to attract greater good into manifestation in your life.

True denial is not primarily concerned with "things," rather with the negative beliefs that bring about conditions that are not in conformity with God's plan for good in your life.

In the process of denial, use definite statements that declare something to be untrue of God, of man, of the universe, of a condition. It is important to remember that denial is primarily an attitude of mind, and it is always the idea back of the denial statement that charges the words with power and does the work of cleansing the consciousness of unwanted beliefs.

Consider these statements that could be used to effectively erase specific error beliefs from your consciousness:

1. If you are holding a thought that God is separated from you, use this type denial statement: *God is my Father, my Creator, and I can never be separated from my Father or His creation.*

2. If you have considered yourself to be limited as a human being, use a denial such as this: *I am not merely a flesh and blood human being, limited to time, space, and conditions.*

3. For a condition that appears upsetting to you, or even frightening, this denial could be spoken: *There is no absence of God's love, power, peace, and protection in this condition.*

It is vital for you to remember that a denial statement cannot stand by itself; it must be followed by an affirmation.

An affirmation is a statement of truth by which you establish in your consciousness the truth about God, yourself, others, the universe, a condition, or a thing. An affirmation is the presentation of constructive ideas by definite words, spoken silently or audibly, in order that the ideas may take hold of your feeling nature, the subconscious phase of mind, and become a possession, yours to have forever.

Just as physical exercise adds firmness and strength to your body, so does the repetition of affirmations with conviction. Making spiritual affirmations is a process of claiming your divine birthright.

Affirmations are the "yes" attitudes of mind that indicate acceptance of your good. Consider these powerful affirmative statements:

1. *God is Spirit, limitless, changeless, Principle.*

2. *There is only one Presence and one Power in the universe, God, the good omnipotent.*

3. *I am a spiritual being living in a spiritual universe, governed by spiritual laws.*

The purpose of affirmations is to build conscious awareness of God. Your affirmations never change God, but they quicken your response to all that is good. As you unwaveringly affirm your good, you allow God by His own unalterable laws to do the establishing or the fulfilling of this good.

As you become better acquainted with your real Self, you begin to realize the vast riches of Spirit which lie concealed beneath the exterior of your mind. Uncivilized tribes may range over a vast tract of virgin soil, seeking pasturage for their flocks and find scant forage; while a civilized tribe may come, observe the same soil, and say, "This will produce abundantly!" and proceed to live prosperously upon the same soil.

Your affirmations are a magnificent claiming of your own good. They represent your divine ideal, the focal point upon which you want your every thought, feeling, and action centered.

So, head straight for your objective by affirming your good, and make that objective the divine outpicturing of the vital life force within you!

Mind Unlimited

You have learned a lot about your mind and how your thoughts can work for or against you. Now, use this knowledge. Obviously, every thought or emotion produces a permanent effect, for it either strengthens or weakens a tendency; furthermore, it is constantly reacting upon the thinker. It is clear that you must always exercise great care regarding what thoughts or emotions you permit to arise within yourself. Never use the excuse that undesirable feelings are natural under certain conditions. Assert your prerogative as ruler of the kingdom of your mind and emotion.

Accustom yourself to look only for the desirable in a person or thing and you will be surprised to learn how many desirable qualities you will find. Set for yourself the goal of constantly thinking good and kindly thoughts. If you do this daily, results will be certain. Your mind will begin to work more easily in admiration and appreciation instead of suspicion and disparagement. Then the thoughts that present themselves will be good and helpful instead of negative and destructive.

"As a man thinketh in his heart, so is he," and it is obvious that the systematic use of thought power will make life much easier and more pleasant for you.

A person who lets himself fall prey to negative feelings is constantly wasting tremendous and precious thought power and throwing away the very thing which can make him healthier and happier.

Every single thought you have, even the most fleeting one, is important. Beware of harboring thoughts of fear, hatred, resentment, sickness, poverty, or injustice. Expel them immediately, but gently, if they try to intrude into your consciousness. Do not fight negative thoughts because this gives them power. Cleanse them with the use of denials and replace them with good, strong, and positive counterparts and you will attract a wonderful life.

Consciousness Conditioners

1. Develop the answer attitude—the attitude of mind that makes you master of life instead of slave.
2. Constantly turn your thoughts toward the spiritual aspects of life and dwell on the infinite good in yourself and in others.
3. Everything you *think*, *say*, or *do* filters through some aspect of your mind!
4. The only thing that can limit the fulfillment of your desires is your own lack of understanding and failure to go forward in Truth.
5. The greatest healer in the world is the golden elixir of vital life force—spiritual energy.
6. It is through forgiveness that true spiritual healing is accomplished.
7. Everyone has a perfectly natural need for loving companionship and you can assert the fulfillment of that need through the answer attitude of love.
8. Action is the indispensable element of success!
9. *Denial* is the mental process of cleansing and erasing from your consciousness all *false beliefs* of the sense mind.
10. *Affirmation* is the presentation of constructive ideas by definite words, spoken silently or audibly, in order that the ideas may take hold of your feeling nature, the subconscious phase of mind, and become your possession.

VII
The Truth about Prosperity

Attunement

Beloved, rest your heart in peace, love, and
adoration on God, Creator of All, and
receive the blessings of the Most High.
Know that God is able to do exceedingly,
abundantly, now and forever. Understand
that as you seek God in sincerity in your
desire to give unselfish service to your
brother man, in like measure shall you find
the greatest gifts of fulfillment and satisfaction.

Is Your Prosperity Overdue?

Search yourself. Are you *afraid* to be prosperous?
Ridiculous question? Not at all. A surprising number
of people want to be prosperous; they want more of
the good things in life, but they are afraid of prosperity. People have asked me, "Is it spiritual to be
prosperous? Is it un-Christian to be prosperous? Why
do I feel guilty about prosperity?" And these are
logical questions.

What Is Prosperity?

Prosperity is a continuous experience in peace, health, and plenty.

For many people, conflicting thoughts about prosperity cause conflict in their affairs. The word *prosperity* means the condition of being successful or thriving; a state of economic well-being. *True prosperity is based on the conscious realization that God's abundance is back of all things.* Material possessions may come and go, but the idea of abundance endures.

Poverty is a "sin." Poverty is a form of private "hell" caused by man's blindness to the omnipresent goodness of God and all substance created by God. Poverty is an undesirable, uncomfortable, unhealthy experience which is unworthy of God's greatest creation—you!

My father and mother taught me that we create our own prosperity. Often we hear people say, "If only lady luck would smile upon me!" Thousands of people believe in luck or fate, but *I believe that you determine your own fate by the way you think, feel, and act.* You *are* your own prosperity and prosperity isn't just an abundance of money; true prosperity is an abundance of all the good things in life.

Mental Preparation for Prosperity

One of the worst mistakes you can make is to put a date or time limit on prosperity or tag it with a label. Prosperity is permanently yours, although it may seem to be delayed in reaching you. Regardless of how old or how young you are, you can expect to experience some form of prosperity. It is never missing from your life.

I am reminded of writing a letter to a friend and anticipating a reply; each day that goes by makes it more likely that I will soon receive a reply to my letter.

If a very wealthy person gave you a blank check—certified, so you knew it was valid—and told you to fill it out for whatever amount you desired, what sum would you use? $1,000 . . . $10,000 . . . $100,000 . . . $1,000,000 . . . or more? To what far-out limits of abundance would your thoughts fly? Do you dare to go the limit and be open and receptive to *all* your good?

Think about prosperity as a promissory note from the universe. All of us have stored up good deeds, kind thoughts, generous actions, and helpful words. These are like putting money in the bank—the interest accumulates. No good we do, have ever done, or ever will do is wasted or lost. Prosperity is our own good coming back to us, if not today, then tomorrow.

Meet Financial Challenges Successfully

Anytime a challenge arises, especially in the form of a financial need, you should know how to meet that need by calling upon your own inner abilities. Often your needs will be supplied in a seemingly miraculous way as were the needs of the Hebrews met. After their deliverance from Egyptian bondage, the Hebrew children arrived in the wilderness. Since there was no food in that barren area, Moses inquired of Jehovah how he was to feed the hungry people. Jehovah replied, "I will rain bread from heaven for you; and the people shall go out and gather a day's portion every day."

Each person was instructed to gather as much as he wished daily, for five of the week's seven days. On the sixth day, each person was instructed to gather enough food for his needs of the day, and for the seventh day also since no manna appeared on the Sabbath. Jehovah's promise was kept, and the people had all the food they needed. Those who gathered little had enough to meet their needs. Those who gathered much had none left over. Each person was free to gather the manna according to his needs and desires.

The Hebrews had been promised a land of their own, flowing with milk and honey—a land of lavish abundance—if they would leave Egypt with all its limitations. This was a hard decision for them, since for centuries they had been enslaved to the Egyptians and believed their source of supply was the Egyptians. In the wilderness, the Hebrews were given an opportunity to prove whether they were willing to look to God as their Source of supply. They had to learn to release old ways of living and old methods of work and accept new ways of living along with new methods for producing prosperity.

After they had proven their willingness to depend upon God as the Source of their supply, one day at a time, the Hebrew children entered a land far richer than the prosperous Egypt from which they had come. By proving their faith in God as their Source of supply, they acquired a firm grasp on the laws of substance. Their understanding increased and they were able to appreciate, wisely use, and enjoy the abundance waiting for them in the Promised Land.

If you find yourself in the wilderness gathering manna, which seems miraculously supplied when needed, rejoice and be thankful. *Know that you are being initiated into the deeper understanding of prosperity.* You are mentally getting ready to accept unlimited supply. You are being freed from fear of lack. As you develop a true, permanent prosperity consciousness right where you are, you will then expand into unlimited good. As you do, your good will not unbalance or overwhelm you. Instead you will be ready to receive it, accept it, and wisely use it.

In many ways you can gather unto yourself the abundant prosperity that is yours for the taking. As you move out of your prosperity wilderness into the consciousness of expanded prosperity that is your "Promised Land," give thanks to God for all you have learned.

Realize, Radiate, and Receive!

You have learned that thinking is the movement of ideas in your mind. Thought is the connecting link between God and man. Your thoughts are the most important tool you can have and use. From these ideas in your mind, you form mental images or pictures (remember thought forms) based on your acquired understanding; these are brought forth as desires and actions. Everything you are is a result of your previous thoughts and feelings.

It is important to analyze your feelings, and to

determine how much *feeling* is invested in your thoughts. What are your thoughts about money? Money is connected by your thoughts to the one Source that is giving or withholding, according to your thoughts about money. Money is good! It is needed for existence in our world today. Your strong desire for money and all good is your success power! How many successful people do you know that are merely "lukewarm" about what they are involved with? How many people who just "don't care" have much to care about? *Right desire* and *strong motivation* are truly the first steps in dealing with challenges and finding the road to greater prosperity. Without a clear feeling for your good, how can you expect it to come about? Desire the highest and the best in life in all areas and you will draw the highest and the best to you.

What is your reaction to thoughts about money? Check out your feelings. Many prosperity blocks are related to feelings such as guilt, fear, resentment, poverty thoughts, lack of forgiveness, thinking of money as evil, and more. You can overcome these feelings by realizing God is unchangeable. But *you need to change* your old negative thoughts into the awareness that prosperity is your spiritual right.

Prosperity is spiritual, and spirituality prospers you in every area of your life. The Bible is a great prosperity textbook. Many "millionaires" are represented therein. Take a look at Abraham, Lot, Isaac, and Jacob. They prospered because they knew God was their Source of supply. They held a God-thought of obedience to the divine laws of prosperity. God is your Source. People, jobs, situations are only channels, and God has infinite channels through which He can prosper you. Get your thinking straight and manifest divine order in your life and affairs.

A friend of mine in the furniture manufacturing industry recently used the law of mind action with successful results. For several months he had desired a certain very fine furniture store chain as a customer and had made every reasonable effort to obtain it. He had made the important personal contacts with the firm and the relationship was pleasant—but unproductive. He decided he would work at building a strong thought form of deliberately and boldly obtaining this account, or a better one.

Each morning, upon entering his office, he quietly closed the door and began to think about that account as if he were already selling it. In his mind, he carefully thought about all the meaningful and beneficial ways his company could serve the client's best interests. He knew his own company's product was superior in quality and would bring good return on the dealer's showroom floor. His daily affirmation was: *I am persistent in my desire for good. I am persistent in my desire to give a good product and good service. I know I will be successful in God's own wonderful way for me. I desire this account, Father, or one better.*

A few weeks later he was attending a furniture market in Atlanta, Georgia, and the president of the firm he had been trying to sell walked into his company's showroom. General conversation led to the two men getting to know each other and the realization that both were avid tennis players. Two days later they were on the tennis courts and a fantastic and beneficial business deal was negotiated. My friend was overjoyed as he burst into my office exclaiming, "It really works! It really works!"

Prosperity Action Steps

1. *Bring your overdue prosperity into manifestation right now by speaking forth definite, positive, and rich words of supply.*

Know that unlimited good is your divine heritage, and it forever awaits your recognition and claim. When you claim it and call it forth, your good will appear.

This prosperity is eternal and ever available. When it seems to have been withheld, the reason is because your own attitudes or actions have obstructed its manifestation; not the attitudes or actions of others, but your own have caused the lack. Speak the word. By affirming Truth, you are lifted out of any false thinking about lack of any kind. Call forth your good.

Affirm: *I see myself in a new way. As a child of God, my resources are unlimited. I rest in the assurance that God provides for my every need abundantly. My action in this partnership is to abide by His law of giving and receiving. An attitude of confidence and joyous expectancy becomes my way of life. God's abundance is being made manifest in my world right now.*

"You will decide on a matter, and it will be established for you, and light will shine on your ways."

2. *Bring your overdue prosperity into manifestation right now by knowing with every atom of your*

being that there is always a balancing, restoring power for good at work in every person, in every experience.

Your good wants you just as much as you want it! Be prosperity-minded. Think prosperously. The world in which you live is an exact record of your thoughts. If you don't like this world you live in, you can change it by changing your thoughts. You can use the balancing, restoring power of change to bring about an improved way of life. As you constantly dwell on the good in every person, in every experience, so do you invite it into your life.

Affirm: *The law of attraction now opens wide every rich channel of supply for me. I invite the balancing, restorative power for good into my life and my every need is abundantly met. I expect the best, and I now attract the best in every person I meet, and in every experience.*

Emerson said, "Great hearts steadily send forth the secret forces that incessantly draw great events."

3. *Bring your overdue prosperity into manifestation right now by using something close at hand. As you use the good you have, be it ever so humble, that good multiplies.*

Prosperity works best when you are optimistic about it. Never say, "I can't afford that!" even if it seems at the moment that you can't. Persist in holding the belief that prosperity is about to catch up with you at any moment—and it will. Believe!

Affirm: *God's divine love, working through universal substance, prospers me and my affairs, making me free, rich, and financially independent. All my needs are bountifully met and I am grateful.*

4. *Bring your overdue prosperity into manifesta-*

tion right now by blessing what you have as you use it with assurance.

Begin to bless your pocketbook and all your financial affairs. Bless your comfortable home. Bless your food. Remember how Jesus multiplied the loaves and fishes by taking them in His hands and blessing them. Something wonderful and mysterious happens when you bless the substance at hand. Since all forms of substance are filled with intelligence, the substance you bless responds to praise and multiplies for you.

Take your present substance, whatever amount it is, and hold it in your hands and affirm with strong faith and conviction: *I bless you with the super abundance of God, the Creator of all there is. Be fruitful and multiply.*

Rich, Richer, Richest

The basic law of prosperity is *give and you will receive.* Sow and you shall reap. For every action, there is an equal and opposite reaction; like attracts like; money makes money; and the rich get richer! You *must* give *before* you receive. You cannot get something for nothing. Start where you are right now. Give of yourself. Open your channels to the omnipresent flow of abundance which is surrounding you, looking for a way to manifest itself into your life.

You can open the door by taking the first step in prosperity—cleansing or purification. Let go of the lesser. You don't need anything in your world except the best life has to offer. Use the vacuum law of prosperity. What is it? How does it compliment the basic prosperity law of give and you will receive? How do you form a prosperity vacuum? Easily—get rid of what you don't want in your life so there will be room for the things you really want and desire to unfold. Nature abhors a vacuum and will rush to fill it. But remember: the goal is to bring forth what you desire rather than the same old things or something less than the best. Eliminate everything you don't need or want from your life, and a two-fold purpose will be served: 1. You eliminate error. 2. You expand your good.

Whenever you eliminate an undesirable, you indicate the belief that something better is on the way. An excellent prosperity affirmation to use in creating a vacuum is: *I now let go of all worn-out things, all worn-out conditions, all worn-out people, and relationships in my life. Divine order is now established and maintained in me and in my world.*

This law of cleansing works so beautifully. Margaret, a student in one of my classes, was preparing to make a cross-country move and was cleaning out closets, storerooms, and every area where "things" had accumulated. She was wavering about letting go a large color console television. Margaret weighed the value of paying moving expenses for the television set or giving it away and purchasing a new one when she reached her destination. Finally she decided to give it to a young couple who had been married only a short time. The couple was excited about the television set and Margaret felt good about not having to move it.

Upon reaching her destination later, Margaret learned that the man who had moved from the apartment which she had leased had left his console color television set with the apartment manager, rather than pay moving expenses. It was free for anyone who needed a television set. She claimed it.

Begin your cleansing process right now by making an *Elimination List* of all things you want to release from your life. Every phase of life requires renunciation for total effective results.

As you clean out the inner, you also clean the outer areas of your life. Look about your home. Begin a prosperity clean-up campaign. Clean out drawers, cabinets, storage areas—every area in your home where greater order can be restored.

Be Deliberate about Your Good

Write down your desires. Write down everything you would like to see "added unto you." Be sure to keep your requests in the affirmative.

Sit in a quiet place and think about the things you would like to have happen in your life. Be specific.

Your *Desire List* is a master plan for your good and can help shape this good into manifestation. After the imagining activity begins, it creates new ways for achievement.

If there is any question in your mind about a particular desire, you can use these four effective checkpoints:

1. Is it legal? Honest? Will it hurt anyone?
2. Is it emotionally right for me?
3. Can I accept the responsibility for this good?
4. What will I let go in order to make room for this good?

Always be certain to place the statement, *"This, or something better, Father,"* at the bottom of your list. You never want to close the door on greater good you may be unaware of, and this statement is the "safety valve" for a higher will than yours to assume control.

Keep your desires to yourself. There is no need to dissipate the energy surrounding your desire by telling everyone. Once you begin to focus your mind, your subconscious begins to believe you definitely mean business this time about prosperity.

There is only one power you can use—God power—and it loves to be used. And that means used, not manipulated. You cannot truly manipulate God power. You can claim your ability to master the rich substance of the universe and take hold of it, therefore, shaping, molding, and forming it with your definite and deliberate thoughts, words, and actions.

Treasure Mapping

The picturing power of the mind is one of the oldest devices known to man for getting what he wants. Someone once said one picture is worth a thousand words and he was right. Picture what you want in big, vivid, detailed pictures. The imaging power of your mind is a strong faculty and it gets results.

An effective method of picturing is called "treasure mapping." This is the action of putting pictures and words of what you want on colorful paperboards. You have the mental picture of what you desire. The physical act of putting these ideas on a physical piece of paper also helps you better organize your thinking by becoming more specific. If you are not consciously picturing what you want in a constructive way, you may be unconsciously picturing in a destructive way.

Specifics for Constructing a Treasure Map

1. Keep your desire to yourself.
2. Use big colorful boards.
3. Use definite colors for definite results.
   (a) Green, gold — financial, job and career success
   (b) Yellow, white — spiritual understanding
   (c) Orange, bright yellow — health and energy
   (d) Pink, rose, red — love, harmony, marriage
   (e) Blue — intellectual accomplishments
4. Use colorful pictures that have a specific meaning for you.
5. Cut out everything, even the words you use and paste them or tape them on your board.
6. Don't clutter your board.
7. Place a money symbol or picture on your treasure map to insure debt-free receiving.
8. Place a spiritual symbol (picture of Jesus Christ or other meaningful symbol for you) on your board and the words, "Thank You, God, for this or something better."
9. Work with your treasure map daily through visualization and affirmations.

Remember—be specific! Generalities do not produce results because they lack substance and power, while a clear-cut picture of the good you want activates people, places, and events to cooperate with your pictured desires. The divine resource of all there is never fails. God is the unfailing resource for all who have faith and who make all their thoughts link with universal Mind. God is your prosperity. Use your ability to think, to speak the word, and stamp this thought daily on your mind. The result will be a more successful and a more prosperous life.

Consciousness Conditioners

1. Get your thoughts in right order for prosperity to manifest itself.
2. Don't place limits on your prosperity. Be open and receptive to all your good through all channels.
3. Use the action steps for greater prosperity:
   (a.) Speak definite, positive words of supply.
   (b.) Change your thoughts, change your world.
   (c.) Utilize what you have close at hand.
   (d.) Praise and bless all your present good.
4. Know the truth about prosperity, and this truth shall set you free from all lack.
5. Start with a "clean house."
6. Nature will rush to fill a vacuum.
7. Help create a vacuum by using an effective prosperity affirmation:
   I now let go of all worn-out things, worn-out conditions, all worn-out relationships, and situations in my life. Divine order is now established and maintained in me and in my world.
8. Be deliberate about your good; write it down. Write out a *Desire List* and an *Elimination List.*

9. Recognize the power of a master plan—it is your divine blueprint.
10. Enhance your world by using "picture power"!

VIII
The Art of Mystical Breathing

Attunement

I am now in the presence of pure Being. I
now behold the living Christ of God in
whose image and likeness I am fearfully
and wonderfully made. I am at peace with
all mankind. I behold nothing but perfection throughout all the universe. I breathe
the fire-breath of God; I live the truth of
God.

The Fire-Breath of God

Breathing is such a natural occurrence that we take
it for granted and we seldom pause to realize its vital
importance. If we don't breathe, we don't live. So
doesn't it seem logical that if we breathe better we
will live better? For centuries in the Oriental countries breathing has been an important "technique"
and a science. These long-ago and present-day sages
realized that breathing is not only necessary but
worth doing well.

Regardless of how well we eat, or what foods we
eat, or how perfect the chemical combinations are,

and no matter how clean we keep our body, inwardly and outwardly, we cannot have a healthy body exuding the proper amount of vitality unless we breathe properly in conjunction with all these other aspects of life.

The air we breathe contains within itself the source of life—an essence mystics have called *prauna*, the fire-breath of God—or that vital energy that is of divine nature, the distilled essence of love. When we breathe properly, we become infused with an intelligence and a special power which activates the physical organism in such a way that, in this complex being called *man*, states of consciousness are produced that we define as spiritual and mental. Thus, the seed of the soul is found in the very air we breathe.

What Is Prauna?

Prauna is the vital energy of the cosmos, the energy often called spiritual energy. Air contains prauna. But prauna is not the kind of matter which the chemist can shove into a test tube, heat, cool, or stare at through a microscope. Prauna is a completely different element.

Prauna, the sacred fire-breath of God, or essence of the Holy Spirit, which is present in the earth's atmosphere as electronically charged light particles of the Father-Mother God, is absolutely necessary for man.

Prauna is essential for the maintenance of life because *it is* the universal energy of everything. It is manifested in everything we can imagine and, yet, we humans use it in the coarsest possible way when we breathe it carelessly and clumsily. Prauna is the divine spark which stimulates our thoughts. In fact, if we don't have adequate prauna in our bodies, there can be no thoughts. The more prauna we can store away, the more vibrant we become with the vital life force, and a greater impact we can make on others.

Gathering Energy

As a child, I vividly remember going for long walks in the fields and woods with my grandmother. As we strolled along, she would occasionally stop and stand quietly, touching the needles of a pine or spruce tree. When I asked what she was doing, her reply was that she was "gathering energy" from these trees.

Conifer-bearing evergreens of the cedar and pine families are believed by many to radiate pure prauna, or spiritual energy. Some doctors recommend that patients who have weak lungs live in the vicinity of an evergreen or pine forest. They believe that pure air, laden with the scent of fragrant pines, has a strengthening and healing effect on the lungs. Many persons obtain this energy directly from the living tree through touch.

Why Correct Breathing Is Important

Have you ever paused to deeply reflect on the act of breathing? Does your daily work require deep thought, the kind of thought where you have to analyze situations and reach conclusions by making decisions? If so, then you might have noticed that as you became more deeply engrossed in thought, your breathing reduced to a slower rate. If you observed an adept during meditation, you would find his breathing reduced to a much slower rate than what we call "normal."

Breath—air—is absolutely essential to each of us. Yet breathing is mostly an automatic function. When our body is resting, breathing is slow and regular. But if we get involved in violent or strenuous exercise, which requires more oxygen to cleanse our blood stream, our rate and depth of breathing automatically increases. It is possible to control our rate of breathing; to slow it down or speed it up at will.

Many sports, such as underwater swimming, diving, and water polo, require breath control. In fact, an American Olympic Water Polo Team trained so it could control breathing under water. One barrel-chested athlete practiced underwater breathing to the extent that he could easily hold his breath for three minutes. Naturally, he was a fantastic asset to his team.

That's fine—if you are a water polo player—but you can master the art of breathing and become very proficient in some important breathing exercises for a much more worthy purpose—to help you become a better person.

The art of mystical breathing has long been associated with spiritual phenomena. Breath was considered to be the conveyance of great spiritual and divine properties, especially as seen with the first breath at birth and the last at death.

Many myths surround the act of breathing. Early Romans believed that it was a religious duty to try to catch the spark of life in the breath so the spirit could continue its existence. The Seminole Indians of

Florida had similar customs. Hindus have made breathing a science, both physically and spiritually. The spiritual and esoteric value of breathing can be traced to the early Vedic literature of India. In those ancient times, when only a few wise ones realized the necessity of deeper and more extensive breathing to clean the lungs of foul air and to bring the blood greater vitality, deep breathing was a religious exercise.

Breathing for Relaxation

The process of deep breathing when our body is resting has tremendous advantages when used for purposes of developing our awareness. The alkalemia which it causes brings a short period of halted breathing which allows our body enough time to relax completely from the efforts of regular breathing, thus utilizing the energy saved for spiritual purposes.

This relaxed breathing also helps us overcome fatigue.

Our respiratory center is a collection of nerve cells which discharge impulses to our respiratory muscles. Thus, we breathe. A deep breath taken during moments of fear, excitement, or other strong emotion helps induce calm.

Spend twenty minutes a day doing the following exercise and you will realize amazing results.

1. Lie down in a quiet place and let yourself relax. Become completely comfortable with no muscles or any part of your body under tension.
2. Breathe deeply and regularly.
3. As you breathe, think in rhythm with the breath-

ing, "Peace, peace, peace!"

4. Allow no thoughts of discord or anxiety to intrude. Concentrate your thoughts upon peace, quietness, and relaxation. Practice will bring you a truly divine sense of peace, and relaxation will flow through your body like a healing balm.

If you will think peace, you will have peace. If you will think relaxation, you will have relaxation. Twenty minutes is a small investment when compared with the fantastic results.

Practice relaxation for short intervals at first, if you find it difficult to relax; you may have a busy mind that won't let up easily and needs to be convinced. Never be discouraged. Each new task is difficult at first, even relaxing. It is only after you can perform a task, and can do it well, that it becomes easy.

Breathing to Start the Day Off Right

A tremendous way to launch each new day is:

1. Upon arising, drink a glass of clear, cold tap water. Do not put ice in the water.
2. Stand before an open window, or go outside if the weather permits; go anywhere you can breathe fresh, clean air, and inhale deeply. Exhale and relax.
3. Stretch your arms horizontally, shoulder high, and separate your feet.
4. Breathe in deeply to the count of five. Hold the breath for the count of five, then breathe out slowly and gently to the count of ten. Be sure your counting has the same cadence for both in

and out breathing. As you breathe in, mentally direct spiritual energy to all parts of your being.

5. Repeat this cycle ten times, or until you feel the invigorating tingle of energy coursing through every cell of your body. It's a great feeling.

I like to use an affirmation with my morning breathing exercises. You might also find it beneficial. Before you inhale, repeat aloud, *I breathe in all the universal cosmic good of God's creation.* Exhale and affirm, *I breathe out all impurities and negativity.* Inhale again and affirm, *I breathe in peace and love and prosperity.* Exhale and affirm, *I breathe out all negativity.*

After performing this exercise for a few mornings and experiencing its effectiveness, you will also find that the affirmations bring you extra benefits.

Breathing to Eliminate Fatigue

The simplest and easiest way to eliminate fatigue and acquire tranquillity is by stretching out, relaxing your muscles completely, and breathing in a gentle, regular pattern. Unfortunately, many people breathe in a "huff and puff" manner and pant along, literally starving their brains of much-needed oxygen. Air isn't rationed! It is one of the few precious free things we have left and there is no reason to misuse it.

Learn to breathe slowly and deeply. It is important to be sure all the stale air way down in the bottom of your lungs is removed. When you breathe only from the top of your lungs, the air on the bottom becomes staler, more unhealthy.

It is only logical that if your air supply is better, your brain power must become better for you cannot live without oxygen, and the brain is the first part of the body to be starved of oxygen.

Think of how you feel when in a close, crowded room. You get tired and sleepy and your movements become slower. It becomes more difficult to think and you might develop a headache. But step outside or into another room where the air is fresh and you perk up.

A regular breathing pattern soothes ruffled emotions. Whenever you are feeling "out of sorts" and thoroughly bad-tempered or over-tired, take a deep breath; the deepest you can inhale. Hold it a few seconds, then exhale slowly through your mouth. Repeat this several times and you will actually feel the tensions and irritability flowing from you.

Let us illustrate the procedure. Draw in the breath steadily and slowly. As you inhale, imagine you are drawing life and vitality—as is truly the case—into your body. Completely fill your lungs with air. Reach out with your chest to make room for more air. Breathe in deeply. Now, cram in a little more air. When you have inhaled as much air as you can, hold it for about five or six seconds—give it time to do a good cleaning job down in your lungs. Then, slowly let the air out so it takes you about seven seconds to get rid of it all. Exhale completely. Squeeze your muscles inward to force out all the air. Then, start over again and repeat the same routine several times. Try it and the first thing you know, the tired, fatigued feeling is gone and you feel happier.

The Purifying Breath

The Hatha Yoga concept of breathing control offers a way of bringing extra prauna into the blood-stream. Probably the most important aspect of breathing, and one which cannot be over-stressed, is learning to use all of your lung capacity. As mentioned before, when you breathe, take the air deep down into your lower lung system and don't stop in the upper chest area.

A simple purifying breath exercise before beginning any other exercise is always beneficial. Here is a good one:

1. Completely exhale all the stale air from your lungs. Push it out until it is all gone.
2. Place your right thumb over your right nostril and inhale through the left nostril for a count of five. Then, cover the left nostril with your right index finger and hold the breath for a count of twenty.
3. Next, open the right nostril and exhale for a count of ten.
4. Immediately inhale through the same right nostril for a count of five, then close both nostrils again for a count of twenty.
5. Exhale through the left nostril for a count of ten, and you are ready to repeat the whole process.

Three or four cycles of this exercise are sufficient in the beginning and you never need to do more than seven complete cycles at one time.

The exercise may sound complicated, but it really isn't and practice will produce a rhythmic procedure which is easy to follow. The purifying benefits brought to your bloodstream are well worth the invested effort. Proper breathing helps rid the blood of its impurities. By holding air in the lungs for a comfortable period of time, you allow more of the creative vitality which it conveys to be transmitted into the blood and deposit its energy.

Three Systems of Breathing

The first system of breathing is called "lower" breathing. Here is how you do it:

1. Sit comfortably in a chair, preferably one with a hard back, with your feet together, your head level, and your gaze straight ahead. Keep your spine erect and your face forward.
2. Relax, and become as comfortable as possible in this position.
3. Take a slow, deep breath, one which will allow the lower section of your abdomen to swell outward, but do not inflate your chest or raise your shoulders.

This type of breath is taken by allowing your diaphragm to sag downward so only the lower part of the abdomen swells out. If you do this "lower" breathing properly, you will find that your ribs do not move. Practice this exercise several times until you become proficient at it. This system allows you to take in more air than the other two.

When you have mastered the lower system of breathing, move on to the method termed "middle" breathing. It is performed as follows:

1. Use the same body position as described for "lower" breathing.

2. Inhale a deep breath while preventing the diaphragm muscles from moving.
3. This time, breathe with the aid of your ribs. Take a great big breath. Notice now that your chest is expanding, but your abdomen remains normal—unexpanded.

Now for the third and "upper" system of breathing.

1. Sit in the same body position as for the other two exercises.
2. Pull your abdomen in slightly as if you were trying to draw it upward toward your chest.
3. While your abdomen is contracted, take a deep breath and raise your shoulders, keeping your ribs as still as possible.

This is a completely different type of breathing and allows the upper portions of the lungs to become well ventilated.

Remember that it is just as important to breathe out properly as it is to breathe in correctly. When you exhale, let your shoulders sag, your ribs close in, and your abdomen push as much stale air as possible from your lungs. It is possible to obtain the maximum amount of fresh, life-giving prauna until you can get rid of all stale air.

Consciousness Conditioners

1. The air you breathe contains within itself the source of life—an essence called *prauna*, the fire-breath of God.
2. The seed of the soul is found in the very air you breathe.

3. Wake up to the vital importance proper breathing plays in your existence and efficiency.
4. It is possible to control your rate of breathing; to slow it down or speed it up at will.
5. Relaxed breathing helps you overcome fatigue.
6. Use the different systems of breathing to bring more life into your living.
7. Begin each day with rejuvenative breathing exercises. You will feel better.
8. It is just as important to breathe out properly as it is to breathe in correctly.
9. Success is achieved by establishing a goal. Start toward your goal and let love be the force which brings the goal into existence. *Love life!*
10. Affirm: *I breathe the fire-breath of God; I live the truth of God.*

IX

Meditation-- the Gateway to God

Attunement

Oh, loving Father, walk beside me. Open the door of understanding so I may become more aware of the Christ, and of His abundant love for all people. As I place my hand in Yours, lead me into doing the simple things that bring happiness and knowledge to myself and to others. Show me how to give wisely of myself and my talents in areas where they are truly needed and acceptable. Let me say with conviction, "I can" and "I will," as my thoughts dwell on the ascending spiral of right thinking, right feeling, and right action. And as "I can" and "I will" become parts of my consciousness, I open the sluicegate of divine power within myself. I walk through the gateway to God.

Meditation Defined

Meditation! What a splendid sounding word—so mysterious and powerful. What thought comes into your mind when you hear the word meditation? Do you form a picture of some scantily clad, little old man sitting in a strange position, in deep contemplation? Meditation, or "entering into the silence," is the wonderful doorway to illumination.

The purpose of meditation is to expand your consciousness Christward and bring into realization divine Truth, and to transform you in spirit, soul, and body by the renewing of your mind.

For many persons the burning question is, "How do I determine what is truly valuable in my thoughts, activities, and daily experience?" Only from within our own beingness can emerge a stable estimate of what is really worthwhile. And this realization is based fundamentally upon each person's understanding of self—self in relation to all others, and self in relation to God and the cosmic universe. Meditation is the productive path leading toward this goal.

What *is* meditation, and how does it differ from prayer? A clear, concise answer is: prayer is when we are talking to God, and meditation is listening for His answer. Meditation is a spiritual attitude. It is a spiritual exercise, a spiritual discipline which enables us to put our mind, body, and soul in excellent condition.

In meditation we attune ourself mentally, physically, and spiritually to the Spirit *within* and *without*, so that God may speak to us. It is simply a process of stilling ourself mentally and physically to *listen*, to really become aware, to feel God's wonderful presence, and to *receive* guidance, strength, and enlightenment. The ability to listen is a part of man's sixth sense. True listening goes far beyond the sense of normal hearing. It penetrates deeply to an inner awareness and sensitivity that transcends the other senses. In this meditational silence we can see, hear, smell, feel, taste, and understand, but on a greatly intensified level of awareness. When we learn the art of meditation, we learn to lift our consciousness to this higher spiritual level.

You Are Divinely Protected

Occasionally someone will ask me, "Can my body be possessed by another entity while in meditation?" The answer is a definite, "No!"

When our thoughts are pure and sincere, our inmost intentions are pure and sincere and we have eliminated fear and replaced it with God's love, then we cannot be invaded, obsessed, or in any way violated. There is nothing ever to fear. When we are unafraid, we radiate a beautiful protective aura which acts very similar to a protective shield. The light of Truth surrounding us also serves as a built-in burglar alarm to alert us about any seemingly negative element.

The words of the Psalmist are a happy assurance of God's loving gift of divine protection to each one of us.

Because you have made the LORD your refuge,
the Most High your habitation,
no evil shall befall you,
no scourge come near your tent.
For he will give his angels charge of you
to guard you in all your ways.
On their hands they will bear you up,
lest you dash your foot against a stone.

Yet, our human intellect tries to tell us that anything as wonderful as *tangible protection from the Infinite* must be earned by much hard work.

Under normal conditions, our physical body is subject to injury and misery through our own accidental or unknowing violations of natural laws. On the other hand, the part of us that is Spirit is divinely protected as God's gift to us, whether or not we ask for this protection. The real of us can never be destroyed! However, physical protection must be earned through adherence to divine natural laws.

The key is that we attract the *personal response* of God to the *love* directed toward Him. We learn how to direct a loving request for protection for ourself. This is a simple exercise, but oh, so powerful in its results:

1. Begin by turning on an imaginary searchlight directly above your head.
2. Let yourself be completely enclosed in a large beam of divine white light which extends out all around you for two or three feet.
3. Recognize the Source of this light as your own highest concept of God.

This protective divine white light is no respecter of person, cult, creed, or religious denomination. It works!

As you are surrounded by your shield of divine protection, *feel* the infinite Power of the divine white light as it bathes you in the highest form of love, love that can best be described as a mixture of beauty and givingness. Let the light penetrate through every molecule of your being and flow like a mighty river throughout, dissolving and washing away everything in your thinking and feeling nature that could act as a magnet for fear.

When you can *feel* the radiance from the white light pulsating in and around you, repeat the following affirmation:

Holy Father, God, thank You for the armor of perfect protection surrounding and filling my being. Thank You for creating a laser-like force field of emotional, mental, and spiritual protection. I carry this protection with me at full strength into all my affairs and daily living. No negativity can touch me. No harm can befall me. No fear can affect me. Thank You for abundant life and illumined growth within an atmosphere of perfect divine protection.

Take this powerful protective shield with you into every area of your conscious activity. It will work for you, and you can build the same protective shield around your family, friends, loved ones, and your personal belongings.

How to Prepare Physically for Meditation

Occasionally we may want to enter the state of meditation, yet find the surrounding conditions nonconducive to meditation. This happens most often as we begin our practice of the art of meditation, but later, as we become more proficient, we can achieve the inner quietude whenever we desire. It is not wise to forgo our meditation period because we may not be in our own sanctum or private place. Any reaching upward toward enlightenment is always successful.

The objective is to become so adept at meditation

that we can make our "attunement" regardless of our physical surroundings.

Try to arrange your regular meditation periods during a quiet time of your day. I prefer early morning, about 5:30 a.m., and late at night; the house is still and quiet and vibrations are good. Early in the day is an excellent time to clear your mind and adjust your attitude for events to come. Evening meditation offers the opportunity to release any possible emotional thought patterns you may have accumulated during times of stress throughout the day.

If you can arrange only one regular meditative period during your day, establish it during the early morning. You should not eat immediately before meditation. You want all functioning parts of your body calm, peaceful, and at rest. In order for the concentration needed during meditation to work freely and without strain, it is important to maintain a balance between the body's physical forces. As much as possible, confine your diet to fruits and fresh vegetables.

Although food plays an important part in helping your body to maintain balance, you should also recognize other essentials for achieving good meditation. A mental attitude of peace, optimism, and perseverance play equal importance in body balance, thereby creating a natural immunization to illness.

Begin and end the day with a glass of water, and drink four to six more glasses of water during the day. If your physical body is to represent the beautiful, well-functioning temple of God it is intended to be, exercise and proper rest also are important.

How to Prepare Mentally for Meditation

It cannot be stressed too often that meditation is extremely important because it wonderfully awakens the mind to higher consciousness and allows the mind to "tap in" more freely to the subconscious. To become adept in the process of true meditation, you may use three vital keys that unlock three important doors. These keys are *sincerity*, *enthusiasm*, and *perseverance*. Let's look at them one at a time.

Sincerity—This is a key only you can use, and no one can loan or give you his. Only you can look deeply into your heart and know the extent of your desire to meditate. You can ask yourself several questions to evaluate your sincerity:

1. Are your intentions sincere in wanting to know what is destined for you?

2. Are you willing to look for areas in your life that need improvement?

3. Are you willing to try to change stagnant areas of your life?

4. Are you considerate and understanding of yourself?

5. Are you willing to put God first in your life?

Enthusiasm—One of the meanings of the word *enthusiasm* is divine inspiration. What a tremendously definitive word! The burning fire of enthusiasm is essential in seeking cosmic consciousness through meditation. Enthusiasm is the inner flame which stimulates every cell of your body and every reflex of your brain to listen, listen, listen.

An enthusiastic person is one who is literally "burning" with firm purpose and is completely convinced of the rightness of his mission. He glows with such infectious radiance that he is magnetic, and he automatically stimulates those who come in contact with his enthusiasm. An aura of authority accompanies his words when he speaks and people listen.

When this enthusiasm is wisely directed, it lends wings to the Spirit, for it is born of the primeval longing of the soul to return to its Creator. When enthusiasm springs from spiritual awakening, every cell of the body cries out, "Here I am! Please take me and direct my path and use me for my highest good!"

How do you develop this spiritual enthusiasm? Study the lives of the mystics. Examine the lives of those spiritual people who, from the beginning of time, found enlightenment and practiced their belief on a daily basis—St. Francis of Assisi, Brother Lawrence, Jesus Christ, and many others. These are all people who walked with God.

Perseverance—This last key, perseverance, is perhaps the most difficult of the three to use. Regardless of how unsuccessful communication may be during the first few days of attempted meditation, you must persevere!

When an overweight person suddenly decides to get rid of excess poundage, he establishes a healthful routine of diet and exercise until the desired weight is achieved. Reaching this goal may require several weeks or months of effort and it requires persistent adherence to an established weight-loss program. In this same manner, *meditation may be regarded as an exercise for the development of your soul*, and if you rush into the practice of meditation like a tourist rushing through a scenic attraction just to say he's been there, your enthusiasm and sincerity will wane.

It is important to practice meditation in accordance with a prearranged program. It is possible to practice too much, just as you might practice too little and end up with a stiff mind—and that is a horrible state of affairs! In the practice of meditation as in all other practices, *balance is the point toward which you aim.*

You can begin your meditation periods with about five minutes each time for the first week. Then, each week, add another five minutes to your meditation period until you reach what feels best for you and brings you the most results.

How to Prepare Spiritually for Meditation

When you unlock the door between your physical and spiritual bodies, meditation helps you become aware of the spiritual forces within. Examine again your inner motives for wanting to unlock the doors to cosmic consciousness and for wanting to embark on a regular meditation program. For many persons, the greatest reason for meditation is to strive to grow and learn in spiritual awareness in order to become a better individual and live a more fulfilling and rewarding life.

When you are positive you understand your motives for meditation clearly, and they are of the highest ideal, then you are ready to pursue the knowledge of accomplishing good meditation.

Most important—whatever your concept of the supreme Creator and the way of enlightenment, *be true to your inner self.* Live the decisions you make.

Live the higher way of life you are seeking. Don't merely say you are striving to accomplish. Do it, and your life will shout to the world the truth of your being.

How to Recognize the "Waiting Period"

In meditation, as with other worthwhile endeavors, you may experience a "waiting period." You have done everything you know to sincerely enter the state of meditation. You have made affirmations, stilled the physical body, quieted your mind, directed your prayer to your higher Self and to God. You are waiting for a response—and seemingly nothing is happening.

Remember perseverance? Patience is another worthwhile and hard to obtain virtue. You are waiting to receive a response or message through a communication line that has not been used before, or perhaps not for a long time, and it is probably all clogged with unsureness, possibly a little fear, and a lot of other mental and physical debris that must be cleared away. Be patient. Persevere in your efforts. Your soul is slowly moving and expanding toward a higher vibration of awareness which is taking place at the unconscious level.

Undoubtedly, this "waiting period" is most difficult until you experience something tangible, but your patience *will* be rewarded. God will not forget you!

During one of your meditation periods, you will be waiting for a response, perhaps straining your awareness somewhat, listening for the unfamiliar sound or impulse that lets you know you are on your way, listening with every single cell in your body. Your whole being is waiting, listening, and receptive, and all at once—it is there! At first you feel that faint, feeble glimmer of response from the cosmic universe.

BREAKTHROUGH! You have reached the secret place of the Most High! You want to hold this manifestation to you lovingly and dearly because a wonderful and rewarding faculty is opening up for you. Your individual concentration, your singleness of purpose has brought results.

As you progress, you may find your preparation process needs an adjustment or change, for the mind needs constant stimulation. If you feel the need to change your affirmation, analyze in detail the meaning of every word to be sure it depicts what you desire to obtain and is a useful aid in helping you focus your attention clearly.

The Technique of Meditation

The methods of meditation can be as varied as the people who are studying this wonderful process. And the various stages of learning can be as wobbly as the first faltering steps of a young child. Learn to direct your conscious attention through sincere desire and to control it through the faculty of will. It is important to maintain the spiritual intent and purpose that you will receive the answer that will be most helpful to your particular request. And the answer you receive may not always coincide with what you think it should be.

When a feeling of peace and tranquillity begins to

flow over you, begin your meditation by selecting one thought or idea. Center your attention within yourself and think about that request you have previously decided upon.

At first, nothing may happen, but if you persevere, as you continue to concentrate upon the focal idea, a faint shaking or trembling may begin within you. Excellent! This faint vibration indicates that the system is working. Then, as you go deeper into a sense of oneness with the creative forces of love, you can listen to the soothingly beautiful inner music that is produced as each psychic center of your body responds and comes alive with the new creative force that is being disseminated.

You might experience a coolness upon your forehead, or a tingle may pulsate along the lower part of your spine. A vibration running up through your body, ending in a quiet sensation of fullness in your head may come, or there may appear to be a sensation or twitching in your eyes. Some have heard an inner voice speaking. Your achievement may come in many ways, but when it comes, hold it closely to yourself and magnify within your consciousness the desire to communicate with the presence of God and receive your special answer from the cosmic universe.

Now, let's learn a simple, basic technique that is guaranteed to bring results when sincerely applied.

All is peaceful, calm, and quiet. Your selected period set aside for meditation has arrived, and you are relaxed in a comfortable position.

Breathe in, and breathe out, slowly and deeply for two or three minutes. This *intentional* act will bring all your attention units to the *here* and *now*. This is useful in itself for we often tend to live our days with a cluttered and confused mind, filled with scattered thoughts. As you become still, your attention will be led from mundane cares and directed toward God and high aspiration.

Now, relax from *conscious effort*. Don't try to visualize anything, or carry on mental discussions, or *force* any kind of result. Be still. Be very still. Let go, and let God bring whatever divine ideas are meaningful to you. Be still with an *open, relaxed, receptive* attitude.

If, during this time, your thoughts wander, think God. A simple discipline of thinking the word *God* will help bring your thoughts back to the central focal point until the habit of staying at that point develops. This discipline is only for the purpose of flowing your attention to the real Source, rather than aimless wandering.

We each have a personal meditation cycle. We turn within, rise to the highest point in perception, then drop back to the stage of awareness. But each time we complete this cycle, we have gone one round higher on the upward spiral of growth. As we practice meditation on a regular basis, our highest point of perception becomes longer in duration.

The *secret* to successful meditation *is to avoid strain*. As you contemplate the highest ideal, with one-pointed attention, the waves of your mind automatically subside. Your mind clears itself. *True meditation is a "beyond the mind" experience—it is your personal opportunity to rejoice in the superconscious realm of divine ideas.*

When coming out of meditation, do it gradually;

don't just suddenly open your eyes, spring up and go dashing off. Slowly let your eyes focus on your surroundings. Relate the inner awareness you have received to outer realities.

There will be a feed-down of superconscious perception; down through the mental realm, the brain, the nervous system, and then into body awareness. The results will be a clear mental perception, a balanced emotional condition, and a harmonious functioning at the physical level. In time you also will notice a smoother, more harmonious working relationship with others and acquire a greater understanding of your total environment. The results: a healthier, happier, richer way of life.

Rewards of Meditation

Meditation brings a tremendous increase in vigor and improved health in all areas. Mastering of meditation brings an expansion of consciousness. And with the expansion of consciousness comes the beautiful realization of your ability to communicate with the cosmic universe and receive results.

You will find a shifting of values from the material offerings of life to the complete selflessness of the spiritual. Yet your material possessions are often multipliable. You will find a greater comprehension and understanding of all things, and a greater sensitivity to the problems and needs of all other living things.

Some students of meditation have the ability to sense any kind of impending danger to themselves or to their loved ones. Decisions seem to be much easier to make. Life progresses much more smoothly because you know the way.

To receive the rewards of meditation, it is necessary to follow the guidelines. Review these guidelines once again. They really cannot be impressed too deeply upon your subconscious mind.

1. *Believe*—for you are a child of God to whom divine power is given.

2. *Relax*—and let your spiritual awareness grow.

3. *Tune in*—be receptive. Look. Listen. Feel. Experience.

4. *Accept*—spiritual guidance in whatever form it is presented.

5. *Act*—on all inspiration received.

6. *Know*—a true cosmic message leaves no room for doubt.

7. *Retain*—what you learn. A continuous effort is necessary.

8. *Develop and expand*—your latent spiritual powers. Reach out to learn more. Seek and you will find greater awareness and deeper understanding.

You will find it helpful to prepare a *spiritual diary* in which to keep a record of your progress and also to write down the important impressions you receive while in meditation. This is an excellent way to retain what you learn.

If this seems repetitious, there is an important reason. You must indelibly inscribe upon your subconscious mind the important steps to meditation and the only way this can be accomplished is through repeating the procedures helpful for you to follow and to persistently practice what you learn.

Consciousness Conditioners

1. Prayer is *talking* to God; meditation occurs when you are *listening* for the answer.
2. Three important keys to effective meditation are: *sincerity*, *enthusiasm*, and *perseverance*.
3. You can build the protective shield of "divine white light" around you.
4. Meditation is the safest, most effective way to understand yourself and communicate with the cosmic universe.
5. Be regular in your meditation periods.
6. Meditation is the gateway to enlightenment and there is nothing more spiritual than a clean body with a clean mind, enshrouding a clean and beautiful soul.
7. Hold a mental visualization of the fantastic rewards of meditation.
8. Awareness and understanding have no limit!
9. Follow the meditation guidelines to success.
10. Keep a *spiritual diary* of the insights revealed to you during your meditation periods.

X

When All Else Fails--Pray!

Attunement

Oh, God, I thank You that You hear me
when I speak, whether the words are
spoken aloud or in my inmost being. Let
me express the true Spirit of my soul. Let
my mouth speak the words that should be
spoken. Let my ears hear the music of the
spheres proclaiming the good in all Thy
creation. Let my eyes behold the kingdom
of heaven come into manifestation on
earth. Let my song join with the celestial
choir in giving eternal praise to You, our
Creator. Let my thoughts ever seek to
know You more fully. May the Christ consciousness be awakened within me this day.
Fulfill in me the promise that I may, in
Your name, do the things that should be
done by me. Come and walk and talk with
me for I am preparing the way. My offering
of love is the gift of myself. From everything less than the perfection of Truth,
make me free. Seal my total being in Yours
with the constant knowing that I am Your
child divine.

147

"I Hunger and I Thirst!"

A man who had come into my office for counseling was discussing prayer with me. He was working through a personal problem and felt he wasn't getting anywhere. He shrugged and threw up his hands in exasperation and said, "I've tried everything I know to try, so I guess it is time to pray." How often I have heard this comment in one form or another. When all else fails . . . pray.

What is your reaction when carefully laid plans fall by the wayside? How do you respond when someone disagrees with you? How do you react when thoughtlessly spoken words hurt your feelings? Do you feel resentful when your mate or good friend calls your fantastic ideas "white elephants"?

When uncomfortable situations arise, remember that even in the stress and strain of daily living, first and foremost you are a spiritual being. You live, move, and have your existence in God and you can act accordingly.

When thoughts and feelings become centered in the external, you lose sight of your ideal; the connection between God and manifestation is broken and a state of inharmony results. This is when you can know the truth about yourself, about others, and about all situations. You can refuse to be misled by appearances and turn toward God in sincere prayer. The wisdom and light of God within you is an unfailing guide. It will direct you successfully when you are open and receptive to its promptings and keep your mind stayed on right action.

Remember that all shadows of ignorance, all false

beliefs, all doubts and fears, all errors become forgotten incidents of bygone days when you hold to the light of Truth.

When you allow God to work through you quietly and peacefully, without worry and strain, you experience the soothing and healing balm of His presence. You react to any person or situation with all that is high and noble. And don't short-circuit your good by over-zealous effort. My son barged in from school one afternoon on the brink of tears because he hadn't done as well as desired in a track meet.

"I'm going to try harder," he affirmed.

"If you do, you won't get anywhere!" I answered.

He stared at me in disbelief until I explained that he was already trying so hard that he was closing off all his circuits through over-intensity. Now, this is not to say disciplines of effort and will are not needed. They definitely are. But the disciplines should be so subtle that they appear as the opposite of discipline. *You want to provide an atmosphere that is conducive to spontaneity.*

Success in life comes when you create the condition of spontaneity—a condition of voluntary or undetermined action or movement—that momentary impulse stemming from the genius of the real you. Other times, you are generating a degree of success called mediocrity. *The real blocks to success are feelings of insecurity, inferiority, and unworthiness, but prayer can remove these blocks.*

You are your own self-starter. As a beloved child of God, you already have everything "built-in" you that you could ever need, and prayer is a powerful key for releasing this dynamo of power.

An Island of Prayer

I often work on the idea of an "island of prayer" in the middle of a "sea of chaos" wherever I am. Why? Because we can lift ourself above the chaos. For example, I enter my office and the telephone is ringing, three people are waiting to see me with emergency situations, the secretary has several important messages, and a list of a dozen things to take care of looms at me from the desk top. Where is the starting point?

I close the door, settle in my chair, and mentally *tune out everything except God and me.* I build a mental island of peace, quietude, and accomplishment all around me, becoming attuned with the presence of God in thought, feeling, and action. I surround myself with the divine white light of the presence of God, and all things cooperate for good— for myself and for all with whom I come in contact . . . and everybody benefits.

This is a good that is tangible, and can actually be realized and felt. When you walk into a room, there is an immediate interchange between your vibrations and those that are already present in the room. Either you have a powerful aura that asserts the comfort and peace you are bringing with you, or the other vibrations of the room—if they are less than the best— pounce on you, or at you. If you are not centered in the light of the presence of God within yourself, you can become overpowered by the intensity of the other vibrations. It is meaningful to build an island of prayer around yourself.

A Power Beyond Your Own

There is a real mystic power, and it works. Know that through your prayer times and your special attunements with God, you are rapidly increasing your own spiritual light. You are building a better way of life in every way and you are attracting exactly what you are building. More light!

Consider this idea: If you are not bothered by seeming negative thinking of others, it is because you are learning to lift yourself above it and tune out depressive thoughts. You are like a television set with all channels functioning. Tremendous energy is in your antenna all the time. You have the power to change the channel selector and receive only one picture at a time—the picture of your choice.

You can "fine tune" the program you really want to watch. This is exactly what you do with your mind. Whatever you immerse your thought power in, whatever dominant mood you give vent to, is what you are tuning yourself into, apart from all the rest of creation. And it reinforces itself.

Naturally, the reverse is also true. When you fall, it is harder to get up again. We are all familiar with this process. If you are around someone who is depressed or extremely negative, the attitude can become contagious if you are not centered in your own strength. One of two things usually happens: either he depresses you or you cheer him up—whichever is the stronger vibration. There is no halfway or in-between area although the reactions may be subtle.

Go forward in the knowingness that there is a larger power available than you are now touching.

Know there is a larger life than you are now living. You are meant for more—meant to do more, meant to *be* more. You look up toward the worlds of space thundering over you. You look within and see the tides of Spirit tugging at your soul. In, through, and around you is power you can feel should be harnessed, power you can realize. It is called prayer power.

Make Prayer a Way of Life

Prayer *is* a way of life rather than a series of isolated acts. It is an attitude of the soul that at times expresses itself in words, but prayer is often best offered silently from within. Prayer is communion, and for communion speech is not always necessary; it is often deepest and most precious when nothing is audibly spoken. In fact, *prayer's greatest degree of effectiveness is when such perfect understanding exists between God and you that words are unnecessary.*

Prayer is the outgoing of your soul toward God in everything it does and says. It is the home-life of the soul; it is the work of the soul, of which the Father is the Source, the center, and the goal. Its eloquence is expressed in deeds and its breath is aspiration. It is as unceasing as breathing and like breathing, it is an inhalation of the pure prauna of heaven.

Nothing in life is foreign to prayer. Everything, both great and small, is swept within its sacred circle. The circumference of the circle includes the remotest province of your individual life.

I know a businessman—a dear friend—who makes a

daily habit of pausing in his work, and for a moment or two he gives his mind and heart the glorious opportunity to dwell on the things most precious to him: his reality as a person, his loving wife and children, and all the good things that life has brought to him. This action quickens his soul, for it is a form of prayer. It makes difficult work tasks easier, consecrates every effort to a more noble use, and produces successful results. *The prayer life is a life of gratitude, made sacred by the intimacy of the soul with its Creator.*

The heart that reaches out and touches God taps a limitless reservoir of the universal substance that Spirit creates, and brings forth abundant supply. *You can't afford not to pray!* When you pray, you get away from personality and come into the great within of you, which is the *real* of you. Then you can bring forth the perfect expression of God.

When an artist forgets himself and expresses God, he paints a picture that comes from within his soul. When a musician forgets himself and expresses God, he brings forth music from within his soul. When an orator forgets himself and expresses God, he speaks with authority and power. The best work is done when you are not dependent upon the personality that may bring forth imperfections. Forget yourself in an attitude of constant prayer. Turn to the great within of you which tells you that you are a child of God and have all the powers of creative mind at your disposal and use. Forget yourself. You may be remarkably surprised at the fantastic abilities the real you contains.

Your times of prayer are truly "food for your

soul." It is through the practice of meditation and prayer that you learn to "practice the Presence," or begin to see God in everything in the universe and, even more closely, you see the presence of God in your daily life. The desire that goes forth from your heart as a hungering after greater awareness is blessed by God and does not return to you void. Prayer does not change God, but it does change your attitude toward Him.

Just as the light pours into a darkened room when the curtains and doors are opened, so does the light of Truth come into your heart when you become open and receptive through prayer. Prayer is like dialing a number on the telephone. It is the *conscious connection* you make with God. You call, He answers.

Asleep on an Anthill

We have often heard the statement, "Pray without ceasing." I wonder if there is any other way. We consciously strive to guard our thoughts without ceasing, to maintain control over our emotions, and to ascertain that our actions are centered in Truth. We are the sum total of our consciousness, so if we center our thoughts on God, we are praying without ceasing.

Thoughts are like ants. One tiny ant may not annoy us; we can easily brush it off and it causes no harm. But if we should fall asleep unknowingly atop an anthill, and hundreds of ants were to swarm over us, we would be much more careful next time.

Prayer thoughts come to us bearing gifts—drops of nourishment for our soul.

Many people give little thought to either prayer or meditation. They seem completely satisfied to drift along in life's currents, waiting and hoping for the proverbial silver platter to drop into their laps. Others sincerely seek a better way of life, continually reaching for the light that brings renewed hope and a better understanding of their position in this earthly life. These are the folks who learn the reason for being placed in this "school" and who work diligently toward graduation.

Prayer and meditation go hand in hand, for prayer is the concerted effort in attuning our physical consciousness to the great cosmic consciousness of the Creator. It is the attuning of our conscious minds to the spiritual forces that manifest in this material plane of earth.

Prayer is communion between God and man which takes place in the innermost part of man's being. It is the most highly accelerated mind action known. Prayer steps up mental action until consciousness synchronizes with the Christ Mind. It is the wonderful language of spirituality, and when developed, it makes you master in the realm of creative ideas.

Your prayers are much more than supplication. *They are affirmations of Truth.*

You never have to supplicate or beg God for the things you need. The important thing is to become still and think about the inexhaustible resources of infinite Mind, its presence in all fullness, and its constant readiness to manifest itself for you when universal laws are obeyed.

When you pray it is important to believe that you will receive—yes, have already received—because God is all that you desire. You simply want to bring your desires into manifestation through the prayer of faith, affirmation, praise, and acknowledgment.

Prayer is not merely asking for something you wish to attain or receive. It is much more than that, and because this is so, prayer should receive careful consideration. Cast aside the temporal and fix your mind on the spiritual and eternal. When you can do this you will find that many items you would have included in your prayer will drop out from the very incongruity of their presence, and the greater and wider issues become to you the focus of your creative powers. *Prayer is highly creative*, and when prayer is offered with this conviction, the objective mind answers to the subjective mind in such a way that an actual creation has taken place.

Are You in the Driver's Seat?

Your Father's help does not absolve you from all thought and effort of which you are capable. God does not work for you but through you. Be aware of the power of prayer and God's help, and be humble enough to receive what is given.

Every force of prayer is a constructive direction and, coupled with power from God, it adds to the creative and redemptive power of light and love to bring about peace. When prayer is uttered with understanding and sincerity it never fails to invoke healing streams of the vital life force from God. It is like setting into motion a vibration that attracts spiritual forces; the waves of awareness of Truth are attracted to the prayer and the person praying, just as steel is drawn to a magnet.

Prayer obeys the one who is in the driver's seat—you. A prayer is your brain-child, your heartfelt desire. It will not accomplish what you wish because you think lofty thoughts or intone a special mantra. It will not accomplish what you wish because you are intellectually wise. It will not do your bidding because you have absorbed the contents of a book. But when you have established authority over your thoughts, prayer will work for you. Not because you command it, but because of its very nature—the nature of the universe compels it, and you are in the driver's seat.

Personal Preparation

For special prayer times, retreat to the seclusion of your personal sanctum. Rest in your most relaxed position. After you instinctively find your right position and the appropriate frame of mind, repeat your prayer sincerely and in complete faith and belief. Then, meditate and *listen* for an answer.

Seven Steps to Effective Prayer

1. Recognize God as Father and Creator of everything.

2. Acknowledge your oneness with God and see yourself as His beloved child.

3. Let your prayer come from the depths of the "secret place" within your heart.

4. Close the door on all thoughts and interests of the outer world.

5. Believe that your prayer is already answered and is now coming into manifestation.

6. Desire the kingdom of God above all else.

7. Free your mind of all unforgiving thoughts. Let go and let God take over.

Let's take a closer look at each of these steps:

1. *Recognize God as Father and Creator of everything.* Look around you. Look at the glorious sunshine; that is God. Look at the fragrant flowers in your garden; these are God. Look at your loved ones; you are seeing expressions of God. Think of the mountains, the seashore, the rolling plains of our great country; here is God. Recognize God as unlimited. There is no place where God does not dwell. Prayer is your process of affirming Truth. If God is present, all situations can be healed.

2. *Acknowledge your oneness with God and see yourself as His beloved child.* Affirm to yourself daily, *I and my Father are one.* There is no place where God leaves off and you begin. Whatever path your life may take, you can never leave the presence of God. Approach your prayer time with the intention of experiencing the presence of God in your life. Truth is individually sought, individually prepared for, and individually received. No effort you put forth is ever lost or wasted. The supreme love of God measures your efforts, exposes your human self, points out errors, shows you God's Truth, uplifts you to Spirit, and takes your body, mind, and soul within His embrace.

3. *Let your prayer come from the depths of the "secret place" within your heart.* The desires of your heart are personal between God and you. There is no

need to voice flowery phrases. Some people pray long and arduously, but I will always believe the greatest prayer of all is, "Thank You, God." The cry from the depths of a distressed soul, "Help me, God!" is more effective and sincere than any long recitation. Asking for something by merely speaking words and relying upon their vibratory effect never helps you become like the Master Jesus. Words contain only that degree of power that is given to them through the consciousness of the individual using them. The true power in your prayer is in your depth of realization of Truth, and your inner awakening of faith in God and the perfect outworking of His laws.

4. *Close the door on all thoughts and interests of the outer world.* This is your special quiet time, and it deserves your full attention. If you are trying to pray for guidance on a problem or situation, but your thoughts are skipping about to various tasks you need to accomplish during the day, you will get nowhere. The same idea holds true here as for meditation. This time is precious. Give it the sincerity and devotion it deserves, and that you deserve.

5. *Believe that your prayer is already answered and is now coming into manifestation.* If you know that your statement of healing, prosperity, or happiness has its basis in the Truth of the cosmos, then you really believe in its validity. Your thoughts receive the impression of belief and act upon it, giving your desire even greater strength. The results that unfold are according to your own consciousness. Don't try to compare, analyze, or draw conclusions from known premises. Let ideas come to you straight from the eternal fount of wisdom.

6. *Desire the kingdom of God above all else.* What you direct your thought power toward is what you will attain. Your prayer is like sending a letter to God. The address is the infinite universe. The return address is your recognition of yourself. The stamp you place upon it—air mail, registered, or special delivery—is your own consciousness of conviction and realization. Your letter reiterates your statement regarding your desires for a better life.

7. *Free your mind of all unforgiving thoughts. Let go and let God take over.* Place your prayer in the stream of the creative action of God. Every prayer addressed to God with a consciousness of faith, love, and sincerity is always delivered. Give thanks that you have the awareness to take the meaningful step of prayer. Then release it lovingly into the hands of the Father and expect results, for results will surely come.

Meaningful Prayer

There are many, many kinds of prayers, including the "gimme" prayers, and the "thank You" prayers. One thing I have become aware of is that God already knows a great deal more about the contents of our heart than we do. Our real purpose of prayer is to keep the contact lines with Him and the cosmic universe well-lubricated and unbroken. The words of a prayer are not as important as some people may think; what is important is the motivating factor behind the words—our sincerity.

Consciousness Conditioners

1. You live, move, and have your existence in God, and you can act accordingly.
2. All shadows of ignorance, all false beliefs, all doubts and fears, all errors become forgotten incidents of bygone days when you hold to the light of Truth.
3. The real blocks to success are feelings of insecurity, inferiority, and unworthiness. *Prayer can remove these blocks.*
4. You are your own self-starter.
5. Tune out everything except God and you.
6. Make prayer a way of life.
7. Nothing in life is foreign to prayer.
8. The prayer life is a life of gratitude, made sacred by the intimacy of the soul with its Creator.
9. Prayer does not change God, but it does change your attitude toward Him.
10. Prayer is creative.
11. Utilize the seven steps to effective prayer.
12. No effort is ever lost or wasted.

XI

Magnificent Manifestations

Attunement

> *Our lives are full of people*
> *who barely move us.*
> *But now and then*
> *we meet impact people*
> *who jar the even tenor of our ways,*
> *knock electrons off our tight little*
> *atoms of living,*
> *and leave us startled, gasping,*
> *growing.*
> *Lord, let the impact of my being*
> *be felt in every life I enter.*
>
> —*J. Sig Paulson*

The Way

When a person begins learning how to swim he often splashes, struggles, and resists, even in peaceful waters. He takes short strokes, works hard, becomes exhausted, and accomplishes nothing. Then he learns that by being calm and turning his face toward God's sky, he can float. Slight movement of his arms will propel him across the water. He has made conscious connection with the Infinite through learning the principles involved in the art of swimming.

Through connection with the Infinite all things are accomplished.

We need more faith and less struggle. It is unnecessary to fume and worry because our plans go awry or because we feel concerned that they may not be fulfilled. One mistake does not have to be followed by another mistake. When we miscalculate we need but to try again, keeping our eyes constantly upon what we wish to attain.

We are here to work out our destiny. If we keep poised and balanced, doing our best every day, realizing that we must under all circumstances be compassionate, kind, and generous with those we meet on life's journey; if we continue doing our best work and thinking our best thoughts every day, we gradually wear away concern over problems, as the swimmer wears away concern of the water. We learn how to meet new situations and this awareness helps us take successful, correct action.

Thus are the channels opened for supply. Thus do we scatter the clouds that obscure the light, and our way becomes clear.

Not by worry and wasted effort and energy do we satisfactorily and quickly accomplish results, but by thoughtful trying and trusting. The divine blueprint for our life is fantastic. It is so much greater than we can imagine. God's plan for us is so great that we glimpse it only occasionally, but these glimpses are the light that leads us through the seeming darkness.

The Basic Life Principle

The great truth and reality of the Christ Spirit in-dwelling each and every soul is truly the basic life principle, and if we always followed that principle, we would become that principle. Would this carry us into a static condition? How could it? It is in this very attitude that we are able to accomplish along a definite line, knowing exactly what we are accomplishing and where we are in life.

Jesus never used a thought that was not turned toward Principle. With that attitude we can all follow in that simple way, not to take something from someone else, but to *bring out from within our own being* everything we need.

We can all work things out for ourself. Once we have solved a problem we have learned the rule. We follow our own course and then we *know* the truth of the Principle. Paths may be presented and different ways shown, but unless we use the way that is best for us as an individual we really don't accomplish our purpose. If we look to others we are adding energy and impetus to something they are doing and we are giving energy from our body. The moment we stand firm within ourself, we add energy to our body and then have ample to spare. This produces a condition that is helpful to everyone. We do not take the thoughts of another to build upon; we build our own thoughts, feelings, and actions into universal conditions that benefit the whole of humanity.

It has been said that no one brings forth an accomplishment in any manner without assisting the entire race of mankind. It is the energy we add, directed in one great attitude of thought, that carries humanity forward. It is not by building upon the other fellow, but by building upon our own foundation. Everything we think of in the name of God, and with that vibration, already belongs to us. This covers all supply, all knowledge, all purity, all perfection, and all good.

We gain dominion just as soon as we put our entire thought on the fact that divinity is already established within us, when we realize that we have only clouded it and thus kept it out of our consciousness by our own adverse thought.

What Are You Doing?

Today, this moment, right now is the only time we will ever have. Tomorrow is for the one who would not now do what can be done. Tomorrow is for the one who is without interest. Where there is interest, there is activity and transformation. How beautifully Paul said this when he declared: "Be not conformed to this world but be transformed by the renewal of your mind, that you may prove what is the will of God, what is good and acceptable and perfect"—*Romans 12:2.*

Will you accept the challenge and the change—and transform yourself?

The earnest person is one who is completely dedicated to the task at hand. There is a simplicity in what we seek to do when we dedicate ourself to the doing. At this moment accept only what uplifts, but don't reject what you do not understand. In a definite change of attitude, embrace all things that are part of you. Then, release—release all and everything.

Become still and know. Know that order, *divine order*, is the high Self expressed through an expanded conscious awareness of you, your world, and your part in it. Make no effort to determine the "how" or "why." Accept. Relax. Release. In this moment there will be an enlargement of you as an individual, and all else and all others will emerge in the light of a new and brighter dawn.

Spiritual development is not the result of a desperate effort to be good; rather it is an inward realization of right which transmutes the whole nature into the likeness of Truth. There can be no transformation in body or affairs until there is transformation within our mind. Expansion of consciousness and greater expression of all that is good result from quiet, contemplative moments of meditation and devoted prayer.

"Mind Stretchers"

As your mind stretches out, seeking, probing, new enlightenment and awareness result. This is the law. Let your mind absorb the following questions and stretch to determine your personal answer. There is no right or wrong answer in terminology, only in understanding and in application.

1. To what extent do you believe that you determine your life and by what means?

2. In building a spiritually conscious expression of life you are given much for your efforts. What is required of you?

3. Give thought to one specific area of your life—your association, your environment, your circumstances, or a condition that is in need of change. What will you do to change this area?

4. How can you always proceed so that you make right choices, without error or regret?

5. You have a mind, body, and spirit that are wonderful beyond comprehension. State specific steps you can take in the development and expression of your mind, body, and affairs.

6. There are many hard and fast rules for freeing ourself from the bondage of ignorance and the chains of self-imposed restrictions. In what way will you discard whatever false appearance prevents others from knowing you as you think, feel, hope, and strive?

7. Without looking up the definition of the word *happiness*, write down what you think it means.

8. List definitive ways in which you can know, give, and experience happiness—ways that you may not have been aware of before.

9. Everyone is sensitive to something. In the poetry of the soul you relate to art, painting, sculpture, sand upon the shore, clouds in the sky, a little child, nature, love, kindness, and understanding. In difficult situations you are also sensitive. These situations may lead to hurt feelings, frustration, and problems for yourself and others. *But the choice is always yours to act or react.* There is a path of simplicity that can make the turbulent smooth. What is it, and how would you specifically apply the means and step forward upon the path?

10. List several factors of motivation that would stimulate you to an action of growth and evolvement.

11. What happens when your thinking faculty is "obedient to Spirit"?

12. If you have faith in God, how can you express this faith to a fuller extent, so that you find greater expression in your life?

13. List several ideas that are to be "wellsprings" of greater good in your life during the next seven days.

14. When is it that the physical, mental, and emotional elements of your being are functioning as one whole?

15. When do you best express your *real Self*?

As you think about these questions, and impressions begin to come into your mind, write in your spiritual diary what you learn or what you feel. It can be another question, an answer, or a realization of oneness with another person or with the Source. Awareness will come to you in many ways. Be alert to recognize new insights.

They Walk in Light

A light burns within the heart of every man and woman. It is the Christ light. The Master gave us glorious instructions regarding how we each may become a child of light.

Ignorance of universal laws, of our divine inheritance, of our inner powers, causes all the pain we experience. Often it seems we stand alone when times of testing, trial, and pain come. There are times when it seems that friends fail us. There are times when plans crash and hopes flee and we sit in darkness. We may brood, shed tears, and wonder why we are in such a predicament.

Then the light comes. The inner light of the soul bursts forth and discloses new avenues, new opportunities, new possibilities. We realize again that it is not in the nature of God to desert us, for He cannot desert Himself and *we are one with Him.* The awareness comes to mind that friends cannot fail us if we have built our friendships on a foundation of understanding. Our cherished plans cannot crash if they are formulated on the principles of Truth. And hope—the visioning of our ideal—can never flee from one whose mind is stayed on the presence of God.

From a scientific point of view there are many octaves of light above those registered by the ordinary human eye. We are constantly surrounded by some degree of light. When the night seems darkest we are surrounded by light vibrations of marvelous brilliance, but we are unaware of these vibrations because we are not responding to them.

By attuning ourself to God, we can raise the rate of vibration in our body atoms so that we can perceive and register light waves of a higher and subtler order, and new wonders will open before our eyes.

They who walk in the light of Truth have discovered one of the greatest realities in the universe. Our soul is constituted of light and in it there is no darkness. Sometimes clouds obscure the mind with impressions of darkness and despair, but the soul of man is ever seeking to arouse within him the realization of his innate glory.

Abdul Baha, the Persian sage, after spending forty years in a Turkish prison, said, *"There is no prison save that of self!"*

Will you believe this Truth? Will you stop struggling against the chains of limitations that bind? Will you give yourself whole-heartedly to the discovery of your inner light?

The glory of God that shone about the ancient prophets was the inner light—the light of God—shining forth unimpeded. Light and understanding have always been synonymous. If you desire to flood your mind with light, it is necessary to train your thoughts in understanding. When you seek wisdom the brilliance of your true Self will be revealed and lo! you will walk in light.

Light is the great reality of God, and you are the great reality of God. Light and you are one with God.

The Splendor of Service

One of the quickest and most thorough ways to unfold spiritually is to be of as much service as possible to others.

A story is told of a monk who earnestly prayed that a vision of Jesus Christ might be revealed to him. After praying for many hours, the monk heard a voice telling him the vision would appear the next morning at daybreak. Before the first rays of dawn appeared the following morning, the monk was on his knees at the altar.

A fierce storm was brewing, but the monk paid it no heed. He watched and prayed that the vision would appear. As the storm broke in great fury, a soft knock came at the door. Interrupted in his devotions, the monk turned away from the altar to open the door. He knew that some poor wayfarer was seeking shelter from the raging storm. As he turned, he caught a glimpse of the vision for which he prayed.

Torn between his desire to stay and see the vision—which he felt would last but for a moment—and his desire to help a brother in distress, he decided that duty must come first. Upon opening the door, he gazed into the bright blue eyes of a small child who had lost her way. She was tired, shivering from the cold, and hungry.

The monk gently reached out his hand and led her into the warm room. He placed a bowl of milk and some fresh bread before her, and did everything he could think of to make her comfortable.

Then, with a heavy heart, he went back toward his altar, fearing that the vision had vanished. To his joy and surprise, it was there—clear and bright and shining with radiant glory! As the monk gazed rapturously upon the precious vision for a long time, he heard a voice saying, "If thou hadst not attended to my little one, I could not have stayed."

It is often said that life is but a day. But let us reverse it and say with a greater awareness that each day is a life. Each new day is a life, fresh and filled with reinstated power, enabling you to go forward on an untrod path of wonderful experiences. You are born anew every time the sun rises and lights up the world. Each new day embodies the fullness of the past, the excitement of the present, and the promise of tomorrow.

When you awaken each morning, resolve that your day will be filled with faithful purpose, loving service, and gentle growth. As the day progresses, throw a glance backward and observe how well you have kept the morning's resolution.

Attaining Your Goal

If you would live the ideal life, you must first enter the hall of divine imagery and gaze upon the perfect pattern which the infallible architect reveals. Life is quickly swallowed up in a world of material attractions unless the image of perfect manifestation of wholeness is constantly held before your inner eye.

Gaze upon your ideal, but then return from your vision filled with the consciousness that you are now what you desire to be. Behold within yourself your own ideal.

Consciousness Conditioners

1. Through connection with the Infinite, all things are accomplished.
2. You are here to work out your destiny!
3. Accept the challenges and changes in life—and be transformed.
4. Concentrate on the thoughts contained in the *"Mind Stretchers."* Write your impressions in your spiritual diary.
5. Love the lessons of life and learn from them.
6. Light is the great reality of God, and you are the great reality of God. Light and you are one with God.
7. When the world seems dark and you are afraid, put your trust in God and smile.
8. Do not allow doubtful thoughts to remain in your mind. Think about the love of God and His

omnipotent good.

9. You may learn the universal laws by seeking. *"Seek, and you will find; knock, and it will be opened."*

10. It is your business to glorify your inner powers and to express them in your own way, according to your highest ideals and greatest understanding.

XII

Breakthrough!

Attunement

Today is the most important day of your life. Today's steps are all you need to take. Today's challenges are all you need to meet. Today's decisions are all you need to make. Tomorrow is the next episode in a great adventure; it will come, heralding its own good. But the present is here *now*. Today you live to the full. Today you exert your best effort. Today you laugh in the sunshine of God's love. Today you savor the sights, sounds, and smells of life. Today you diligently apply all lessons the past has taught you to living in the now. Today is your opportunity to serve, to love, to understand, and to grow in cosmic consciousness. When today is finished, lay it gratefully aside. Thank God for today's unique experiences, for there will never be another day like this one.

The Voice in the Wilderness

When I climb to the summits of majestic mountains covered with stately trees towering above daisy-speckled meadows, I find around me breathless beauty. When in awe I behold vast quiet reaches of desert—golden sands flowing to meet sky-blue waters, I am touched with the majesty of creation. When I stand on a rocky cliff by the ocean and watch the tide come and go, I feel the presence of God and recognize my oneness with Him.

Our beautiful earth is a place where birds sing, animals and children play, the sun shines, and rain falls. It is a special place. It is our home.

Is it a better place because you were born?

Different countries have their own stories and legends, and there is an old American Indian myth which goes like this. When a tribe member made the journey through the doorway to another life called "death," before he could go forward in the new life, he had to face the Great Hunter and answer one question affirmatively: Was the earth a better place because you were born?

As a child, I remember my parents saying to me, "Wherever you are, whatever you do, make earth better because you passed through."

As the present is heir to the past, so will the future be the child of the present. The present is where you are *right now*. You can fearfully anticipate the future or you can make a conscious effort to build a better future, which means that you work today with a positive attitude and begin shaping your world right now in the manner you desire for tomorrow.

A skeptic may object by saying, "But with our recent history of wars and hostility and in view of the present world situation, is there any reason to believe in civilization and to be optimistic about the future?"

Absolutely!

Remember that you are living in an age in which men have walked on the moon. You are living in an age when research in consciousness is rapidly gaining momentum. You are living in an age when more people are being born than ever before. You are living in an age of communication between planets. You are living in an age when people are seeking and finding the presence of God in their personal lives, even amid the tension of our present society. Man's divine spirit is getting tired of residing in turmoil and confusion. Humanity is ready for enlightenment.

You do not live in a time of decline, but in a time of transition. Think about this: not a time of decline but a time of transition. The world often may seem at odds and appearances may seem hopeless. Not so!

Even the darkest night must relent before the approaching dawn—the coming of the new day, and *we are living at the beginning of a new day . . . a new age . . . an age that some call "golden."*

The shocks and upheavals of our time are but the storms of a forthcoming spring which sweep away what is decayed to make room for the newer, the better. These are but the growth pains of a new era, an era that gives birth to a race of men and women who are strong and supreme because they are united in one cause—mankind's evolution.

Just as the powers from the depths of the earth push out violently to the surface in the form of volcanoes, so are the great powers and abilities coming to light in the souls of men—souls who have been shaken by growing pains and who have had to overcome great obstacles.

The new world does not begin in the outer, rather it comes from within each one of us.

We have within us the power and ability to bring forth new life. We have within us the power and ability to be stronger than anything that distresses, grieves, or tries to limit us. But it is necessary to recognize and affirm this recognition through courageous action. Right now is the time to ask yourself: "What action am I taking? How many people are happier because I was born?"

As a child of God, what has your birth into this civilization, on this planet, meant to the happiness of others? Have you sung a happy song to our earth? Have you picked a perfect rose and given it away, just for the sheer joy of giving it to someone? Have you taken the time to cheer someone who was sick? Have you shared your food with someone who had less? Have you inspired the discouraged or brought a joyful smile to the upturned face of a child?

Will our earth be richer in happiness because you passed through? What enduring moments will you contribute to humanity? A house built . . . a child born . . . a tree planted . . . a family raised . . . a caring ear when someone needs help? What expression of your mind and spirit will be remembered?

Will you give words of faith, hope, and love? Will you give acts of thoughtfulness and kindness, or present an example of good character and noble living forever to influence your family, your friends, and the people you meet every day?

You have been born. You are here. What you think, say, and do will become a part of all those whose lives you touch.

"But I'm only one person," you may say, "and my voice is that of one crying in the wilderness."

Yes, that is true to a degree. But a government is made up of persons and operated by persons. Countries, cities, families—large and small—are constituted and run by persons. We each must do our share.

Have you done your share to bring about peace? When you maintain a peaceful attitude, there is no way a quarrel can begin between you and another person or thing. The greatest and most destructive wars were fought because somewhere along the way, at some point in time, one person—someone who was a leader, made a decision to fight.

The largest business and the biggest industry came into manifestation because one person had a dream and a good idea that worked. A starving country is fed because one government official had an idea of sharing food and he put the idea into action.

We are the ones, you and I, who clear the way for a bright and glorious future. You and I, with our intense desire to make a better world, are the hope of glory and perpetuation. You and I are important. Our words, deeds, and thoughts either add chaos or spread the healing balm of peace. World peace begins at home, within the heart of every person.

In Your Soul You Are Free

Oh, mankind, how lovely you are in your God

identity. Jesus Christ said, "Blessed are those who hunger and thirst for righteousness, for they shall be satisfied." The moments of your infilling with increased spiritual awareness are thrilling beyond belief. Your soul gasps in divine anticipation that it might receive a breath of the reality, that it might perceive the loving presence of God reaching through all experience and gently beckoning you to move forward into a greater expression of cosmic light, with the fullest degree of confidence.

The day arrives in the heart of every seeker after Truth when he stands tottering on the threshold of a new life. He has walked and worked among the same old scenes, but in some marvelous manner, he has renewed his mind by cleansing away old error thoughts and embracing new inspired ones. He desires to free his body of any weakness or limitation and come into the realization of the perfect health he envisions. He begins to understand that his Source of supply is the infinite reservoir of Spirit, and that he has the option to draw upon it for all his needs.

You, magnificent pilgrim, are standing at the entrance to a new life—new because of your new thoughts that have turned from the darkness to the Light. You may find that this new life is not easily entered because of the force of attraction to old, straggling thoughts. But you are now a greater thinker than you once were. You have discovered the power of *will* and *imagination*. You have discovered that by conscious effort you have attained the strength and ability to overcome any opposition and to create new conditions. You have the power and ability to build surroundings more in harmony with your new Self.

Your every prayer for perfection is an appeal for the greater expression of the glory of God. Be aware of the hope that blazes throughout the portals of space, awaiting an opening into the doorway of your heart.

Dream the Possible Dream

Who are the dreamers? They are the souls who are the architects of the world's greatness. Their futuristic vision lies seeded within the rich soil of their adventurous souls. The dreamers never see the limiting mirages of so-called fact. Their vision can peer beyond the veils and mists of doubt and uncertainty and pierce the walls of time.

Makers of empires have fought for bigger things than crowns and higher seats than thrones. They are the "Argonauts," the seekers of the priceless fleece—the Truth. Through all the ages they have heard the voice of destiny call to them from the unknown vasts. Their brains have wrought all human miracles. In lace of stone, their spires stab the old world's skies and with their golden crosses they kiss the sun.

They are the chosen few—the blazers of the way—who never wear doubt's bandage on their eyes, who starve and chill and hurt, but who hold to courage and hope because they know that there is always proof of Truth for those who try. They know that only cowardice and lack of faith can keep the seeker from his chosen goal; but if his heart be strong and if he dreams enough in sincerity, he can attain the goal, no matter that men have failed before.

Walls crumble and the empires fall. The tidal wave sweeps from the sea and tears a fortress from its rocks. The rotting nations drop off from time's bough and only things the dreamers make live on. The dreamers are the eternal conquerors and their vassals are the years.

Are you a dreamer? You are one of the chosen because you have chosen to grow and express. You have chosen to give forth your energies to seek a better way of life. Be renewed. Be reborn into the magnificent life of Truth. Invoke your own shining star—the star of the Truth of your reality as a child of God. You can become a light which the shepherds and kings follow to the birthplace of the Christ, over and over and over again. You can so fill the universe with the light of your radiance that mankind can be guided to the place of divinity.

Let your light shine!

Cosmic Credo

A credo is a statement of belief. Perhaps the realities expressed in this credo will become living words for you.

I BELIEVE that there is a divine blueprint for my life. It is etched within the folds of my being, even as the rose is wrapped in the bud. I believe every soul born into the world has a mission; that mission does not consist of "doing this" or "accomplishing that," since it would then be at the mercy of circumstances. That mission consists of being true to the highest aspect of the real Self. The divine blueprint can be followed successfully in whatever situations I am

181

placed. *Life is no accident; it is a sacred trust.*

I BELIEVE in God. I believe the glorious Fountainhead from which we draw all our good is the omnipotent, omnipresent, and omniscient Source of everything, the Creator of all there is—God. I am the director for all my good . . . joy, strength, peace, health, and an abundance of every manifestation. In order for this manifestation to occur, I must direct my thoughts, my emotions, and my actions to living in harmony with the great universal laws. The good I give out must then, by these great laws, return to me as my own manifested good.

I BELIEVE in the power of thought. It is stamped on the face of every man, woman, and child I encounter. I can read the habitual thought of the individual plainly impressed upon the countenance, the figure, the gait, the gestures, the writing, and the speech. *What dwells in the soul of each person is expressed in every part of his being.* I can follow the Master's example of positive thinking and helping others by wise and friendly encouragement.

I BELIEVE perfection and wholeness are God's desire for all his creatures. Singleness of purpose, living in the light of Truth, will enable me to become a pure channel for a joyous life. It is important for me to live in harmony with Spirit. When I do this, I can go calmly and peacefully about my way, keeping harmony always in my daily life and keeping peace always within my heart so that the neighbor, friend, family member, and all those among whom I pass, are also lifted up.

I BELIEVE in the most powerful element of God, that great cohesive force that holds every atom of the universe in its proper place, and it is called *love*.

Love in the Divine Mind of God is the expression of universal unity. Love is the magnetic attracting, harmonizing power that enfolds everything in perfect order.

I grasp a comprehension of love as it is clothed in form. I see love manifested in man as tender compassion between husband and wife, the infinitely tender relationship between parent and child, the devoted service for a cause one believes in, and as kindness and unselfishness toward all creation. I see God's love manifested by observing the divine order throughout the universe. The relationship of our sun, moon, stars, planets, flowers, trees, seas, and mountains are all expressions of love manifesting through Divine Mind.

I BELIEVE in the law of growth, for the law of growth is the law of expansion. It is the law of life, giving expression to the inherent, dynamic urge for fulfillment of the divine plan for man and all creation.

I BELIEVE that use is the law of increase. If I use what I have, it will increase. If I use my talents, faith, and knowledge of my oneness with God, I will grow and expand in consciousness. But it is better to take one idea, assimilate it, and truly understand it, than to try to acquire all knowledge at once. As new depths of awareness are plunged, I must use this new knowledge in *responsible* service for God to others.

I BELIEVE that the Christ Spirit within me is my hope of glory. The Christ consciousness within me is the living, vital presence of God right within my own being. God is the power, presence, and intelligence within that I can claim to transform my life. I know I am not just a body with a mind which is ruled from within or without, but both body and mind can be made obedient servants to the Christ Spirit.

I BELIEVE the key to power is the *knowledge* that I am a child of God and heir to all His good. When I can stand steadfastly and unwaveringly with my eyes fixed directly on that which is true, knowing and seeing nothing else, I hold a powerful key. I am made or unmade by myself. In the armory of my thought, I forge the tools by which I can be crushed or uplifted. I have the power and ability to bring forth my ideal.

Transfiguring Affirmations

My goal is God. I start this day with God by taking my first thought of His Presence within my own being. This is a free-will offering to my own God-Self. I recognize the divine spark and I desire to fan it into a brilliant, blazing, eternal flame of light and Truth.

God, I am united with all universal life and power, and all of this strength is focused in my nature, making me positive with Your perfect energy to send out to every form. This energy is so positive that it transforms all into harmony and perfection. I know that all is in accord with infinite life, freedom, and peace in God.

My mind is fully polarized with infinite intelligent wisdom. Every faculty of my entire body finds free expression through my mind, and all humanity expresses the same wisdom.

God is all life. I am inspired with life by every precious breath and it fills my bloodstream with vitalizing energy.

Father, my heart is filled to overflowing with the peace, love, and joy of the conquering Christ Spirit. I see in every face that same conquering Christ Spirit. My heart is strong with Your steadfast and perfect love, and I know that it fills the heart of humanity. God-life enriches my entire world eternally *now.*

I am supreme mind. I am supreme wisdom, love, and power. From the depth of my soul, I shout the glad thanksgiving that I am reborn into the perfect power of the supreme Mind of God. God, I am!

My Father and I are one. My Father-Mother Creator—God—and I are one!

Consciousness Conditioners

1. Today is the most important day of your life! There will never be another day exactly like it.
2. Is the earth a better place because you were born?
3. We are living at the beginning of a new day, a new age, a time of transition to a higher state of consciousness.
4. The new world does not begin in the outer, rather it comes from within each of us.
5. In your soul, you are free. You are free with the freedom of Spirit. Soar to whatever heights your dreams can carry you.

6. Life is no accident, but a sacred trust.
7. That which dwells in the soul of each person is expressed in every part of his being.
8. Live according to your credo!
9. You are one with God and can never be separated from Him and His good.
10. Your human body can do no more than submit to whatever design is imposed upon it. Follow your divine blueprint.
11. Your mind is designed to be your guardian angel.
12. The Truth shall set you free!

PUBLISHER'S ANNOUNCEMENT

Breakthrough! is published by Unity School of Christianity, an independent educational institution devoted to teaching the principles of Christianity and the application of these principles to everyday life and affairs. In addition to *Breakthrough!* Unity publishes the following books:

Atom-Smashing Power of Mind, *by Charles Fillmore*
Be! *by James Dillet Freeman*
Be of Good Courage, *by Frank Whitney*
Be Ye Transformed, *by Elizabeth Sand Turner*
Beyond a Miracle, *by Sue Sikking*
Both Riches and Honor, *by Annie Rix Militz*
Charles Fillmore Concordance, The
Christ-Based Teachings, The, *by Donald Curtis*
Christ Enthroned in Man, *by Cora Fillmore*
Christian Healing, *by Charles Fillmore*
Consent, *by Newton Dillaway*
Dare to Believe! *by May Rowland*
Dynamics for Living, *by Charles Fillmore*
Emerging Self, The, *by Ernest C. Wilson*
Focus on Living, *by Winifred Wilkinson*
God a Present Help, *by H. Emilie Cady*
God Is the Answer, *by Dana Gatlin*
God Never Fails, *by Mary L. Kupferle*
Gospel of Emerson, The, *by Newton Dillaway*
Great Physician, The, *by Ernest C. Wilson*
Guidelines for a Healthy Marriage, *by David Goodman*
Guidelines for Parents, *by Anne Lee Kreml*
Halfway Up the Mountain, *by Martha Smock*
Happiness Now, *by Mary Katherine MacDougall*
Healing Letters of Myrtle Fillmore, The
Healing Now, *by Mary Katherine MacDougall*

Health, Wealth, and Happiness, The Prayer Way to, *by Lowell Fillmore*

How I Used Truth, *by H. Emilie Cady*

How to Let God Help You, *by Myrtle Fillmore*

How to Use the Power of Your Word, *by Stella Terrill Mann*

Inside Me, Outside Me, *by Elizabeth Searle Lamb*

Jesus Christ Heals, *by Charles Fillmore*

Keep a True Lent, *by Charles Fillmore*

Know Thyself, *by Richard Lynch*

Lessons in Truth, *by H. Emilie Cady*

Let There Be Light, *by Elizabeth Sand Turner*

Light for Our Age, *by Robert P. Sikking*

Like a Miracle, *by Sue Sikking*

Live Youthfully Now, *by Russell A. Kemp*

Magic of the Word, The, *by May Rowland*

Magnificent Decision, *by James A. Decker*

Make Your Dreams Come True, *by Stella Terrill Mann*

Master Craft of Living, The, *by William L. Fischer*

Meet It with Faith, *by Martha Smock*

Metaphysical Bible Dictionary, The

Mind: the Master Power, *by Charles Roth*

Mysteries of Genesis, *by Charles Fillmore*

Mysteries of John, *by Charles Fillmore*

New Age Understanding, *by Donald Curtis*

New Unity Inn Cookbook

Only Believe, *by Sue Sikking*

Open Your Mind to Prosperity, *by Catherine Ponder*

Patterns for Self-Unfoldment, *by Randolph and Leddy Schmelig*

Practical Christianity for You, *by James E. Sweaney*

Prayer: The Master Key, *by James Dillet Freeman*

Prospering Power of Love, The, *by Catherine Ponder*

Prosperity, *by Charles Fillmore*

Prosperity Now, *by Mary Katherine MacDougall*

Revealing Word, The, *by Charles Fillmore*

Revelation: the Book of Unity, *by J. Sig Paulson and Ric Dickerson*

UNITY SCHOOL OF CHRISTIANITY
Unity Village, Missouri 64065
Printed U.S.A.   136-F-2265-10M-6-77